LILITH
GODDESS OF DARKNESS AND LIGHT

LILITH
GODDESS OF DARKNESS AND LIGHT

SPECIAL EDITION

DAVID THOMPSON

* TRANS MUNDANE *
PUBLISHING
—— OCCULT KNOWLEDGE ——

A Legal Disclaimer:

A Warning:

This is very powerful material. When worked properly, you may see unexpected results. These rituals and petitions are like electricity, the energy will flow in the direction of the intended output. In saying this, please be firm in your intentions and make absolutely sure what you want is truly want you desire.

As they say, be careful what you wish for, you just might get it.

To Adsila.
Who fully embodies the Goddess

"Magik: The Science and Art of causing Change to occur in conformity with Will." - Aleister Crowley

Part One 1

Introduction... 3

CHAPTER ONE 5
My Background with Lilith 5

CHAPTER TWO 11
Lilith Creation Myths.................................. 11

CHAPTER THREE 21
The REAL Lilith 21

CHAPTER FOUR.. 25
The Magick of Lilith.................................... 25
Curses and Baneful Magick.......................... 26
Goddess Magick.. 27
The Key to Making Magick Work.................. 28

CHAPTER FIVE 31
The Basic Ritual.. 31
Pathworking the Rituals............................... 34
Basic Pathworking to Daemoness Lilith........ 35
Your Desire... 37
Getting Answers with a Pendulum 38
Preparing for the Rituals 39

Part Two..43
The Magick of the Daemoness....................... 43

CHAPTER SIX.. 45
Ritual for Answers 45

CHAPTER SEVEN 49
Sex Magick 49
Basic Sex Magick 49
Pathworking Sex Magick.............................. 54
Sex Slave Ritual.. 55
To Return a Lost Lover (Against their will) 64
Return of a Lover Pathworking...................... 68

CHAPTER EIGHT 70
Protection Magick.. 70
Pathworking Protection................................ 74
Mess 'Em Up 76

CHAPTER NINE... 81
Revenge.. 81

Retribution 86
CHAPTER TEN 90
   Cursing 90
   Curses! Curses! 91
   A Basic Curse 93
   Destroying a Business Rival 96
   Destroy a Relationship 100
CHAPTER ELEVEN 105
   New Money Channels 105
   Money Bags Ritual 110
Part Three 115
Magick of the Goddess Lilith 115
CHAPTER TWELVE 117
   Lilith the Goddess 117
   Ritual for Answers 118
CHAPTER THIRTEEN 121
   Success Magick 121
   Success in Business 125
CHAPTER FOURTEEN 130
   Rituals for Money 130
   Basic Money Magick 130
   Money Bags Ritual 134
CHAPTER FIFTEEN 139
   Love Magick 139
   Basic Love Ritual 140
   Strengthening Love 145
   Reuniting with a Lost Love 148
   Reuniting with Friends 153
   Aura of Glamor 156
   "Piss or Get Off the Pot" (AKA Make Him/Her Commit)
.... 161
CHAPTER SIXTEEN 167
   Protect Children 167
   Safety for your Partner/Spouse 170
   Healthy Childbirth 173
   Success in School 177
CHAPTER SEVENTEEN 183

Healing Magick... 183
Physical Healing 184
Healing Emotionally 188
CHAPTER EIGHTEEN.. 193
The Sigils 193
Daemoness Lilith (complex).................................. 195
Daemoness Lilith (Simple) 197
Goddess Lilith 199
Goddess Lilith (Simple).. 201
Protect Children 203
Protection Sigil... 205
Money Draw 207
Compel Sigil 209
Success Sigil 211
Appendix.. 213
Helpful Links 213
Oils... 213
Misc Items:... 216
The Pendulum 216
Pendulum Charts 218
Banishment 221
About The Author 224

PART ONE

LILITH

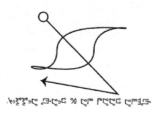

ᐴᐅᕈᕐᐱᐣ ᒍᐨᒐᐤᐸ ᙭ ᒍᓐ ᖕᙯᙯᕐ ᕿᓐᑐᐱ᙮

DAVID THOMPSON

INTRODUCTION

In the pages of this book, you will find a collection of rituals to Lilith, in both her form as Daemon and in her form as a Goddess.

A collection of over <u>TWENTY-FIVE</u> rituals for Lilith. Not counting the pathworking versions of the rituals, and by far the most rituals I have ever written for a single Goddess or Daemon.

This is because Lilith's powers are far ranging. Lilith's powers are empowering to anyone who asks her for favor.

And, for the first time, I also include what some would call "baneful" magick. Use these rituals with caution. Her magick is quite powerful.

On more than one occasion, someone has asked, "What do the Daemons get out of helping us with magick?" Or it has been "boogieman" myths from someone trying to scare people away from working Daemonic Magick, saying how the spirit that is summoned will either possess the magician or "steal" all their energy. This results from traditional religious upbringing, in my opinion. A hold-over from the puritans who had all these behavior rules for their followers. It's an attempt to control others, because the person making these comments is frightened by anyone else who takes control over their own life.

So, what DO the spirits get from this? Honor. Attention. Recognition of their existence and magick. *Belief!* In other words, they get the energy that comes with belief.

Gods, Goddesses, Daemons, Daemonesses, Genius Spirits, all of them, exist off of the energy they receive from us, through our beliefs in them. The energy from the offerings and sacrifices. A single drop of our own blood has energy, a lot of energy. That single drop.

That is what they get. They will rarely ask for more. A god may, just to keep you on your toes, ask for a more expensive offering, like a rare liqueur.

The ancient and elder gods also wish people to recognize their existence. They have existed for a lot longer than the currently recognized gods. They want you to know they're here for you, and they don't require all the annoying days of prayer, or other trappings demanded by certain "approved" gods and saints.

CHAPTER ONE

My Background with Lilith

This book results from working with Lilith for years.

In my book, Daemons of High Magick, in the chapter on Lilith, I had forgotten that I'd worked with Lilith a few times previously before my more recent workings with her. (I'm revising that chapter, BTW)

She is very powerful. A force to be reckoned with, and a force you can have in your corner.

This book will also deal with the subject of using magick to force someone to act against their own free will. I'm sure this will alarm plenty of people, but the magick associated with Lilith is often quite dark. Plus, I figure it's good to have this type of magick in your back pocket for times when you have to deal with people who just won't stop harassing you or a loved one. Over the years, I have had plenty of people decide I was a target and start trying to harm me. I didn't start it, but I sure finished it.

For when I first worked with Lilith, I'll have to go back several decades. In the mid-1970s, I'd read a witchcraft book with a section for men. In this section was a complex ritual to subjugate a woman as a sex slave. This was the first time I'd read about such magick. There were several spells that also used Lilith, so I attempted to work one (to attract sex, of course!). It failed. So, I thought seriously about the subjugation spell. I talk about that one in the chapter on Sex Magick.

My next use of Lilith magick was in 1985 when I worked a minor spell to get back in touch with a young woman I'd lost contact with, and this was in the days of having to change phone numbers every time you moved. I was in the mid-cities of the Dallas-Ft. Worth "Metroplex", and had lost contact with a beautiful model that I wanted to photograph again.

I'd found a small book on spells and witchcraft, and in it was a quick spell that used a pink candle, a pink ribbon, and - of all things - a cigar. It was a very easy spell to work.

The spell asked Lilith, classified as a "daemon" in that particular book, to reach out and put the practitioner in contact with someone they thought was lost. This was sanctioned under the Wiccan creed of not working against anyone's free will, because the spell was written to make it so that paths crossed and the rest was up to the magician. The target is not forced to seek anyone out. This ritual used a pink candle, pink ribbon, and a cigar.

One afternoon, fresh from a stop at a local tobacco shop at the mall, I had a cigar. On the table was a pink candle, the ribbon and my intention. I'd written out the spell on fresh paper as instructed, and I worked the spell.

I recall it worked pretty quick. A new bar/nightclub had just opened, and I decided to drop in and check it out. After my eyes got used to the dim lighting, and my ears somewhat dulled by the onslaught of mid-1980s dance music, I spotted a tall woman with bright blond hair, making her way across the room, holding a drink tray. It was the young woman I'd worked the spell to meet again. Working as a waitress in this new club.

She remembered me, and I got her number. In a week, she was over for a photo shoot. I maintained contact with her for quite a while after this "chance" meeting.

My next workings that used Lilith were years later, in the 1990s, after I'd been married, divorced, and was living in Texas. I used a version of the pink candle spell to see to it that someone who owed me some money would appear and make amends. In this case, it was a model who was paid in advance, but then flaked out on the scheduled shoot. Again, this spell worked. This one used a variation of earth magick and was a bit harsher as it asked Lilith to "haunt" the target until they made contact.

Once again, this person contacted me. I was renting an office in a large studio in downtown Austin and two models walked in. I was only expecting one, but she dragged along a friend visiting from out of town. Guess who the friend was? Yes, that woman. She also told me she'd been thinking about me and had even seen me in an education video that I was involved with during my 1988-1991 years in Los Angeles. Fast forward to the following weekend: both women were on a boat with me for a photo shoot.

Then, in a few more years, I used Lilith to deal with a crazy guru woman, which I'll cover in the chapter on Protection Magick.

After another pause for several years, then I began thinking about Lilith. I'd recently moved to Los Angeles, and was launching my side gig of doing readings and rituals for others. A man contacted me, wanting me to figure out a way to pry his lovely daughter away from the abusive boyfriend. While in meditation, a goddess appeared, walked right up to me while smiling. It was Lilith. She transmitted the information to work a ritual for this client, and to ask her for the assistance.

I worked the ritual, and the last I'd heard, the boyfriend had been picked up for DUI. The police stop also uncovered that the daughter was obviously a victim of physical abuse from this guy.

After that, off and on, I've used Lilith for all types of rituals for clients. During this time, I purchased the only statue that seemed to say "Lilith" to me. Not the copy of the Mesopotamian statue of Lilith, but a small angel statue. It was far more fitting for the goddess I'd come to know. It is a small, bronzed statue of a nude female with wings, sometimes titled "Kneeling Nude Winged Female Statue".

I have continued to work with Lilith anytime I, or a client, have an issue she can address. This book results from all my experiences with Lilith as a goddess and as a daemon.

In my past High Magick books, I have touched on some darker magick, or "Baneful" magick, but in this book, about half the daemonic rituals call upon Lilith's darker side, her baneful magick.

Allow me to address that subject here. The "Law of Return" is a modern Wiccan thing which appears to have its origin in mid-20th century religious dogma. Possibly something from someone's Protestant background. I have only experienced a negative "blow back" on the occasion when I used the sex slave spell. That is likely a lesson I had to learn myself, taught to me by the powers I called in the ritual.

Negative return is a dogmatic concept and isn't real. Unless you really believe in that, then you will experience some type of blow back when you work a piece of magick to harm another. The best thing to do is ask Lilith to deal with the target, as she is a very compassionate, caring spirit, even in her aspect of Daemoness. I have found that she will deal with the target in a manner most fitting to their actions against another. Especially when it comes to abuse against women or children.

However, I have added the use of black salt to minimize any "blow-back" effects of these rituals.

The pathworking rituals, when included, will follow a set pattern, but the visuals will vary depending on the type of desire. As I'll point out later, not all rituals in this book have a corresponding pathworking ritual. However, using the general pathwork steps, you can use that technique with any ritual.

Now, get ready for an experience as you experience the magick of Darkness and Light.

CHAPTER TWO

Lilith Creation Myths

One of the more entertaining myths about Lilith, mostly found in the older Abrahamic religions, is that Lilith was created alongside Adam in the garden. Lilith proved a bit too much for Adam, demanding to be his equal, thus Adam complained to Yahweh. An angel was dispatched to deal with her. An argument ensued, and Lilith stormed off.

This angel was again dispatched to locate Lilith and drag her back to the garden. Instead, Lilith had discovered Jehovah/Yahweh's sacred name, and used this to take control over the angel, and basically told everyone to "Feck off".

Perhaps it's easier to read this as a short fantasy story, set in premodern historical times.

***

12,756 BC (approx.)

Tuesday, April 19th. 8:17am. Eastern Garden Time.

The tale of Lilith begins in the Universe Creation Lab, currently in use and run by the Creator God Jehovah, approximately twelve thousand Earth years before the modern era began. He received special permission to run an experiment in a little used area of the planet Earth, as long as he put everything back once he was done. (*We all know how that worked out.)

The seraph fluttered nervously as it approached The Boss. This seraph was one of the multiple winged angels, with eyes everywhere. They were tasked with keeping an eye on things. Or several eyes, as the case may be. It cleared its throat and ruffled some flight feathers.

God finally looked up from designing a small mammal and frowned. "What do you want now, Caliel?" He asked.

"It's the human you made," the angel said, visibly nervous.

God grunted and turned back to His creation. He placed a second webbed foot onto the creature carefully, and sat back, a smile on His face. "What do you think?"

"Uh, what is it?" Caliel asked.

"I'll call it the platypus." Another smile as he turned the animal around. "I used all the spare parts we had left from the beaver project. Plus, some additional left-over parts from the avian test labs."

"I can see that," the angel said under its breath. "It is cute, Lord."

"Yes, that's by design. My next idea is something even cuter. It'll make you want to hug it and scratch its stomach, but then I'm going to add sharp, pointed barbs all over its back. Purely defensive, mind you." God smiled, then he focused on the angel. "What now?"

"It's that human. He's going after the sheep, again," Caliel reported.

God sat back and sighed. "I should have made a pair of them to start with." God stood up and shook his head. "Best show me what Adam's doing."

The room spun and twisted, and in an instant, the Creator and the angel Caliel stood in a lush jungle clearing. God watched for a moment, then spotted the human running naked across a pasture, chasing a terrified sheep.

"Is he killing them and eating them?" God asked.

"No," Caliel sighed. "Just watch, sire."

They watched as the human finally caught the sheep and twisted it so that it was on its back. God grimaced as the animal's bleating reached his ears.

"He has all the self-control of those rabbits you made last week, which is none!" Caliel said, watching the human wrestle with the sheep.

"Alright. I've seen enough. I guess I have to make another one of those humans and see where it leads. We'll have to use the existing pattern; I have done nothing with the design in a while. Have the engineers meet with me in the lab," God ordered, then vanished.

Caliel looked back to where the human was raping the animal. The angel shook itself, then vanished, leaving behind a few gray feathers.

***

Garden of Eden (V. 1.2)

  A few days later.

Adam looked in disgust at the woman. There was just something off-putting about her. Her attitude, she insisted on doing everything he did, and her refusal to engage in the sexual acts he preferred, often forcing herself on top of him. Hadn't God told him he had dominion over all living things? Yes! And that command included this woman.

God had assured Adam that, given enough time, this creature would come to love him and eventually submit to his rule.

Adam figured enough time had passed, and now Lilith wouldn't even consider doing that thing with her tongue anymore. She said it tasted funny.

To make matters worse, she'd insisted on adopting a small canine as a pet. She carried it everywhere, even though it had four functioning limbs and was capable of movement on its own.

Lilith sighed and sat on a small rock, then started feeding the furry animal berries. She'd stop picking them for that monster man Jehovah had made. He was smug, saying that he was made first and, because of that, he made the rules. Lilith considered that the man was made first, and thus had suffered from multiple design flaws and serious mental issues. Lilith was made in perfection, with multiple improvements in both physical design and software.

"Have you changed your mind?" He asked.

"I might. If you do the same to me," Lilith replied, returning her attention to Mister Sniffles.

"Not even if you washed it first, would I dare use my month upon your lower regions," he replied, wrinkling his nose at the thought.

Against her own will, Lilith watched the man's face. She was still struck by his beauty. Still rough around the edges, but she figured with enough time, she'd get him to change. She tried to imagine what he'd look like with some extra hair along his chin. She sighed again.

"Then I'd have to say no," Lilith said.

***

Upstairs, so to speak, Caliel rushed back into the lab to find God tinkering with a few sea creatures. He watched as the new bivalve design tested its locomotive methods. It shot across the virtual ocean floor and God leaned back, smiling.

He turned to the angel. "Now, that's what I call traveling in style." God frowned at the seraph, who was visibly shaken. Turning back to his work, God said, "Okay, tell me what happened."

"Sire, it's the male human. He's screaming and crying,"

Caliel reported.

"Oh, what now?" God grumbled. He turned to the angel and said, "What is it this time? Did he injure himself?"

"No, he's saying the woman has left him."

"Now, why did she do that?"

"I looked back across the timeline, and it seems she's very forceful, wanting things her own way, and then they had a huge argument this morning." The angel consulted a small scroll. "She has escaped from the Garden by climbing a tree and getting over the wall."

"Damn," God mused. "I know we used the usual off-the-shelf designs."

"Lord, it's that free will," Caliel reminded Him. "If you recall, many of us advised against it."

"Nonsense. These creatures need a sense of freedom. Even if it has consequences," God argued. "Only way for them to learn, you know."

"That's just setting them up for failure, Boss."

"Okay, enough! I know what I am doing, you know. Send down a messenger, and have it drag that woman back into the test enclosure."

"Send who?"

"Send Gadriel. It's time he takes an interest in the garden experiment. Have him return that woman back to the enclosure. That's an order," God said, turning back to the ocean view, only to see a predator fish gobbling up the new bivalve. The crunching of the shell was loud. "Oh, damn you!"

With that, the predator froze and slowly sank out of sight.

***

Down in the garden lab, a more traditional angelic being appeared. Gadriel looked around and spotted the human male seated on a rock, its face in its hands.

"Where did that female go, did you see?" Gadriel asked. Adam just shook his head and pointed.

"Fine. Whatever," Gadriel grumbled and began hiking to the area where the male had pointed. He easily spotted the tree that the female had used to get across the wall. Eyes narrowing, the angel levitated to the top and stood, scanning the horizon. Fertile pasture land as far as his eyes could see. But no sign of a human.

Caliel materialized next to Gadriel. "You find that woman, Lilith?"

"She's nowhere to be seen," Gadriel said. "You have a look. You have better eyes. Certainly, more of them."

Caliel gazed out towards some towering mountains in the distance.

"Oh, I spotted her. There, near that grouping of trees," Caliel said, pointing.

"Right," Gadriel said. "I'll go deal with her." He lifted the hem of his white gown as he stomped out onto the grassy plain, muttering, "damned apes. What in the universe was He thinking?"

***

Lilith leaned against a tree, basking in the shade. Mister

Sniffles busied itself digging at a root, trying to make as big of a mess as possible. The Watcher appeared in a pop of light, which sent the little dog into a fit of barking and growling.

"I don't think he likes you," Lilith said, looking at the angel. This one was different. It was more "human" but with wings.

"You need to come back with me," Gadriel said. "Without the noisy animal. Lord God Above is displeased with your actions."

"Ooo. Ask me if I could care any less," Lilith said, lifting the dog. He had stopped barking, but was still eying the angel and growling.

"It's His command. You are to return and do as Adam commands," Gadriel insisted.

"No," was all Lilith said.

"You fail to understand," Gadriel said, getting angry. "God, our father demands it. He has ordered you to return."

"I don't think so," Lilith said, nuzzling her dog, then she looked up at the angel and smiled.

"He demands it! Now come with me!" Gadriel demanded.

Lilith just smiled. She looked the angel in the eyes and began muttering. Gadriel's eyes narrowed. What was this human up to now?

Gadriel opened his mouth to order the human to comply, but he found himself unable to move, much less talk.

"In the names of El, Elohim, and Eey Oh Yeah, I command thee to leave me alone. Be gone!" Lilith ordered.

Gadriel was suddenly back in God's Creation lab, looking confused.

"Did you handle it?" God asked. Gadriel just looked stunned.

He slowly shook his head.

"Can't you speak? Talk!" God demanded.

"Your Holiness! I could not move! She muttered some words, and I was here!" Gadriel explained.

"Impossible. She's not an immortal. Of anyone, I'd know that!" God pointed out. "So, tell me what happened!"

"I'll tell you," Lilith said, her voice echoing through the lab. God's eyes narrowed as he looked for the source of the voice.

"I know your sacred name, you old fraud. I used it to banish your Watcher, and I have found myself able to perform all sorts of miracles!" Lilith appeared in a small cloud of vapor.

"Then I banish you! I curse you and your kind!" God shouted; his voice punctuated by the rumble of thunder.

Lilith laughed and vanished.

"What just happened?" Gadriel asked, quietly.

"A mistake. A big one!" God grumbled, and dug through some scrolls. He grabbed up one and peered at the writing.

Caliel rose from his hiding spot under a lab table. "I heard all that. What is she?"

"A goddess! A damned goddess! See? Right here," God's finger stabbed at a line of writing. "Whoever transcribed my formula used a Delta code, and not an Omicron code. Delta codes are only for Watchers and Seraphim, not humans!"

God's eyes narrowed. His face grew red as he fumed.

"You mean we created a goddess?" Caliel asked.

"In her case, a demon! Let word go out. Lilith is a demon! She is cursed!"

Henceforth, and throughout history, Lilith was no longer seen as Adam's first "wife", but as a daemoness.

***

And that, gentle readers, is why Lilith is a daemoness. Maybe.

CHAPTER THREE

The REAL Lilith

During my work with Lilith, I am able to channel her energy and from that contact, I have managed to see what her origins actually were.

During the periods prior to civilization, as defined by archaeologists (meaning settled tribes and using agriculture to form the basis of cooperative living) men in the northern parts of Europe marched south, conquering the tribes they encountered along the way. These people, run by warlords, brought with them the patriarchal religions, which focused on men as the Sky-Father, with deities such as a pre-Zeus "yaus-pater" deity. Along the way, they encountered a number of matriarchal and earth-deity (chthonic) religions (Greece, Middle East and associated areas) or organized religions with very active gods and goddesses (Egypt) and naturally the Old

Gods of the conquered lands became the demons up to no good and the invader-gods became the heroes combating the demons.

Many of these original gods were Immortal Masters from lost civilizations.

But many deities were not. These were spirits who were, literally, created by these people and imbued with immorality, what we in magick call an "egregore".

Unlike a goddess such as Aphrodite, Fortuna, or even Astaroth, Lilith is a true "egregore", a spiritual creation of the people of her time. Soaking up the energy the worshipers offered, multiple gods and goddesses arose in these early days of our current historical time line. This was a period long after the echoes of the destruction of Atlantis had died, and civilization was struggling to restart, having forgotten the amazing technology and history of the previous civilizations.

I asked Lilith to show me her real origins, not the rabbinical myths. I initially got images of fertile farmlands, lush green foliage, buildings made from quarried rock. Buildings now long, long gone.

The fertile crescent, the confluence of the Tigris and Euphrates rivers, land of the Sumerians. This was about 3500 B.C.E. The people of this time worshiped multiple deities. One of these goddesses was the handmaiden of Inanna. Babylonian texts say, "Inanna has sent the beautiful, unmarried, and seductive prostitute Lilitu out into the fields and streets in order to lead men astray." The name "Lilitu" has been said to be the original name for Lilith.

The images I get from Lilith showed her being attended to in temples set aside for the pleasure of men, temple prostitutes. She showed me she was sometimes worshiped as the patron goddess of prostitutes. This appears to be the origin or her amazing powers when it comes to sex magick.

She informs me she results from many "Lilith-type" daemons coming together as one, in the late 1700s. It appears many magicians all at once began using Lilith, rediscovering her ancient magick of lust, sex, and subjugation.

Lilith appears in Goethe's 1808 work Faust Part 1, where Mephistopheles explains to Faust that Lilith was Adam's first wife. It was in the art and literature of the 19th century, and then into the occult world as a daemoness, with this invocation of Lilith:

Dark is she, but brilliant! Black are her wings, black on black! Her lips are red as rose, kissing all the Universe! She is Lilith, who leadeth forth the hordes of the Abyss, and leadeth man to liberation! She is the irresistible fulfiller of all lust, seer of desire. First of all women was she - Lilith, not Eve was the first! Her hand brings forth the revolution of the Will and true freedom of the mind! She is KI-SI-KIL-LIL-LA-KE, Queen of the Magic! Look upon her in lust and despair!

(*I use some of this invocation in these rituals*)

A well-documented life. Multiple myths, the blame for the "Original Sin", without which the mainstream Western religions would have had to make-up another excuse for making women subservient.

CHAPTER FOUR

The Magick of Lilith

Lilith is a goddess who can tackle most any request, from protecting children, up to and including, the subjugation of an enemy.

However, before I go much further into her magick, a word of warning. Like Kali, Lilith will deliver to you your desire, even though the desire itself will manifest in unexpected ways and sometimes delivered with a lesson. Treat her magick with respect.

Another thing: Lilith doesn't care about the usual restrictions on free will. She will subjugate people for you, and make people act against their own free will. Especially with love magick! For example, if there is a soul contract in which a particular person is supposed to be with you, but they're too scared to commit, you can compel them to be with you. The long-term results may not be as good as you'd want, however.

Her preferred method is to use her magick to enchant those around you, making yourself much more attractive. Called "Glamor Magick" and this is quite effective.

Her magick has been seen to break-up relationships which have turned toxic, freeing the abused partner. In one instance, she went off on the abuser and the guy wound up in an accident, then in jail. All I'd requested for my client was that Lilith break up that couple. She did the retribution on her own.

Lilith exercises her free will as a Goddess like no other deity or being that I have ever worked with. I use her magick with caution, and it's often just enough to have her take a look at a situation and simply deal with it in a manner that would please everyone involved.

I have split this book into two major parts: Daemoness Lilith and Goddess Lilith.

I give you the basic rituals for each aspect, then I go into the specific rituals I have found to be very effective.

Curses and Baneful Magick

For this, we will use Daemon Lilith. It's the aspect of Lilith that is the subject of quite a few books already. A few words of caution are needed before you dive into this aspect.

Blow-back, or negative results, are a real possibility when working any baneful magick. The targets have to really deserve the attentions of Lilith. A good example is when someone is abusive towards another, then the abuser deserves Lilith's wrath. Someone in a position of power who abuses their subordinates needs a good curse put on them.

But make sure you are ready for what Lilith may do. You may find working with Lilith an exhilarating experience, or you may be horrified at what happens.

Goddess Magick

Empowerment is the keyword when working with Lilith.

Lilith as a Goddess is as powerful a being as you'd ever want to summon. She's direct, works quickly, and will give you honest feedback about your desires.

She excels in Love Magick, because of her roots as a goddess of family. As a deamon, she can make a desired person come to you against their will, but as a goddess, she can charm them into actual love for you. However, she may advise you to work magick to make yourself desirable, and you may find your preferred partner is someone other than the person you were originally crushing on.

Success is easy when you ask Goddess Lilith for help. If you are up against unfair competition (which is common in our current environment), you may find it necessary to work the baneful magick against the competition, then the success magick for yourself.

The Key to Making Magick Work

Often, the simple act of summoning a powerful being like Lilith will be enough to make the magick work. Sometimes, it takes a few small additions.

Our minds are separated into two distinct halves. The left hemisphere is the "Rational" mind, and the right hemisphere is the "Irrational", or creative side. Also nestled inside our minds is a small section, usually in the left hemisphere, which I call "Doubting Debbie" (or Doubting Dan). Think of this section, and its voice, as the "rational" relative or friend you may have, the person who thinks nothing is real unless they can touch, taste, smell, eat or screw it. Magick functions in an area outside of the physical. So, that part of your brain may look around, then say, "Hey! Wait a second! That can't work! Magick isn't *real!*" That doubt will stop any magick from working. Period.

The only real way to shut up old Doubting Debbie is to *show* her that the magick actually works.

"Gee, Dave. How the heck do I do that?"

Easy. Start small. Follow each step.

Especially the step which says "*Meditate a few minutes and visualize the outcome.*"

You don't need to spend hours in a special meditation, making humming noises or staring at a blank wall, usually holding your hands in a special way. No.

But you need to be familiar with the altered mental state called "Alpha".

This is a state where you allow yourself to gently relax, like your mental state, when you just wake up. Dreamy. Some call it a daydream state. Others call it gnosis.

The key to getting into this state is relaxing. I have been doing this stuff for decades, so I can "drop" into alpha most anytime. Even in loud, crowded airports.

At first, relax yourself by reclining back, and begin sending thoughts to each bit of your body, like your feet, ankles, and legs. Next, your upper legs, hips and lower back. Then relax the back and neck, shoulders and down your arms. Then up your torso and into your head. Let yourself relax. Just feel this relaxed state.

If it helps, obtain a meditation audio at 10 Hz, the brain frequency of alpha.

That quiet, calm state, nice and relaxed, is the "Alpha State".

While in this state, Doubting Debbie is somewhat muted.

You take control of this mental state when meditating. Then visualize how you see the magick appearing. See your desire manifesting! Go into this daydream, and experience the desired outcome!

I worked a ritual for a new car. While in meditation, I saw a car. I saw its shape. The color was a metallic green. In six weeks, I saw the car again, except this time it was maroon, and a salesman was opening the door and handing me the keys.

So, I cannot emphasize this enough. Fully visualize the magick manifesting your desire. See it happening. There is no need to feel any emotions. You don't have to "match emotional frequencies." Just see it happening. Then, trust in Lilith to make it happen.

CHAPTER FIVE

The Basic Ritual

As with all ritual magick, there are certain steps and ritual items one needs to accomplish the job. For Lilith, when doing a physical ritual, you'll either be calling on Lilith as a daemoness or goddess. The requirements for each are different.

I have simplified the rituals quite a bit, as many of the trappings of a regular ritual to Lilith are just extra fluff. Some rituals also have pathworking rituals. Not all, as some types of magick essentially need a more formal ceremonial ritual.

When working a ritual to the Goddess form of Lilith, you will need:

1. Altar Candles in Pink and White for Goddess Lilith
2. Incense as stipulated in each ritual.
3. Offering bowl

4. Symbol of Goddess Lilith (or a nice statue)

5. Heavy wine glass if offering wine

6. A lighter to light the candles

When working a ritual to the Daemoness form of Lilith, you will need:

1. Altar Candles in Red and Black for Daemoness Lilith

2. Incense as stipulated in each ritual

3. Symbol of Daemoness Lilith or a statue.

4. Sterile Lancet for drawing blood.

5. Fireproof bowl for burning the offerings

6. Lighter for the candles.

7. Black salt (recipe in Appendix)

8. Oils (various, recipes in Appendix)

Offerings will vary depending on which aspect of Lilith you are summoning. For the Goddess aspect, go with fresh flowers, fruits, sweet breads, honey, cream, etc. The Daemoness aspect prefers a drop of blood on her sigil, then the paper is burned. Alternately, you can use an unbroken raw egg, a small bit of beef, or strong spirits such as whiskey.

Altar candles should be dedicated to only Lilith. I like the small 3-inch by 3-inch round candles. They're easy to set up, and I have drawn her sigil onto the set of candles I use. When covering a ritual candle in oil, some rituals call for a specific oil, others just say "oil". In that case, use any mineral oil. Try to avoid using olive oil, as it's pretty sticky. Mineral oil is easy to find in the US and it's what I use.

Incense. I have had students in the past who can't burn actual incense. I shared a condo with someone who went absolutely bonkers if I burned actual incense. Not because she was allergic, but because she was against my magick workings. I would have to work late at night, with windows open, so I could exhaust the incense. That's also when I began developing various meditation or pathworking rituals.

When working a physical ritual, try to have as much of the ritual items as possible. You can substitute some items, but not all. The sigils are absolutely necessary. They can be hand drawn, but it's best to print them out and use the prints. Lilith's new daemonic sigil is quite complex, so I have also supplied a simpler one for use on her candles. The same with the goddess sigils.

One step in the ritual is to banish negative energies. I have a short page on that in the appendix.

In the ritual steps, I have you pause several times. One is to look for any signs Lilith is nearby. This can take the form of any number of manifestations: Candles flickering "funny", incense smoke streaming against a draft, swirling, and up to actually seeing her appear. If you do not see any of this, rest assured, Lilith will be with you in these rituals. I have her word on that!

Pathworking the Rituals

Not all the rituals have corresponding pathworking rituals. And some rituals are only pathworking rituals. In magick that requires the more "formal" rituals, there will be no pathworking with it. This is as Lilith has wished it.

I'm playing fast and loose with the term: "Pathworking". These are mental exercises, designed to attune your energy to that of Lilith, in either her Goddess form or her Daemoness form. Not the type of pathworking usually associated with magick. Each one is different, and each one is tested.

You have to visualize scenes, and as you imagine each section, your energy will shift, and this shift will open up the channels between yourself and Lilith. With each pathworking, it is vital that you visualize the shielding of golden light when working the paths for Daemoness Lilith. This simple exercise will shield you from any beings who might want to enter your space while working the darker rituals, because while working the darker rituals, you are aligning with an aspect of Lilith that differs greatly from her Goddess form.

You begin these rituals by making sure you will not be disturbed, and you are comfortable. Some people sit in a meditative pose, others in a comfortable chair, and even a few who will lie down on a couch or bed for this work. It's best not to work these rituals immediately after eating or drinking, as this might cause some noises or effects which will pull you out of the meditative state.

Have this book open to the ritual you wish to work and have

a printed copy of her sigil.

If possible, play calming music, something with no background "beats", as these will cause your brain to sync with the beats and possibly drop you into a deeper meditative trance state than needed for the pathworking.

Once comfortable, turn off the cell phone and anything else that might cause noise. Those with children, do your best. When my daughter was very young, I worked magick only after she was down for the evening.

It's okay to open your eyes and refer to the book during these rituals. You can also work these in darkness, by the light of a single candle.

Do whatever works best for you.

Basic Pathworking to Daemoness Lilith

This uses any sigil you have created for your desire. Make sure to have it with you physically when working these steps.

Once you are ready, sit and allow yourself to relax.

Imagine a golden glow starting in your heart area.

This glow expands to completely surround your body.

Imagine yourself at the edge of a thick forest.

The sun is suddenly covered by thick clouds.

A huge owl glides overhead.

You find yourself on a forest path.

The owl stares at you from a tree branch.

Talk to the owl. The owl represents Lilith.

Send some energy to the owl, giving thanks for assisting you.

Pick up your sigil, and ask Lilith to appear.

She will now appear near the owl. Hold up the sigil, and ask her to activate it, to bring this desire to you.

In your mind, hold up a white rose, then prick a finger and let a drop of blood fall onto the rose.

Give this rose to Lilith. Tell her how grateful you are.

You now turn around and walk out of the forest, along a path.

As soon as you exit the forest, the ritual is done.

Basic Pathworking to Goddess Lilith

Contact Goddess Lilith by visualizing:

A bright day, clear blue sky above.

Green grass spreads out under your feet.

A clear bubble appears in the blue sky above you.

It drifts closer. And closer.

It turns bright gold in color, solidifying.

Goddess Lilith appears in the golden light.

She smiles.

You now say, out loud or in your mind,

"Goddess, I thank you for coming to my aid.

"I ask that this now occur."

Speak aloud your desire, like a petition.

Go into a daydream and see your desire manifesting. Go

into detail.

Focus again on Lilith.

To thank Lilith, visualize PINK light appearing near your heart.

This PINK light activates the petition and sigil if you made one.

At this point, give thanks to Lilith for assisting you by sending her some of this pink light.

She will now vanish, leaving only an outline.

In your mind, turn around and walk away from the scene.

Open your eyes. Take a few moments to return to fully awakened consciousness.

This ritual is now competed.

Your Desire

A major part of any magick practice is the preparation of a petition, a statement of what you want the magick to accomplish. Although, one can summon Lilith to simply ask her questions, especially if you are having issues distilling your desire into a simple, past-tense statement.

I have had Lilith give me a sigil for a desire. The design just arrived in my mind. The sigils in this book were given to me by her for use with the rituals in this book.

When thinking about what you wish to accomplish with Lilith's magick, you need to make a self-assessment of not only what you want, but how it might arrive. It is a good practice to ask a daemon to join you, and communicate to you what ritual might work best, how to phrase your petition, and what offering to give.

I will work a pre-ritual summoning to a daemon that I haven't worked with in the past just to ask questions and receive answers. I am somewhat "gifted" with the ability to hear spirits, so I can receive their answers quite easily. But what about if you have trouble hearing the spirit?

Then get a pendulum.

Getting Answers with a Pendulum

In the appendix, I have a copy of part of a class I gave, where I taught the students how best to use a pendulum. By using a pendulum, even one you made, will allow the daemon to clearly answer your question. The use of an alphabet chart, the daemon can spell out the answer, and even guide you to the best statement of desire.

In the links in the Appendix, I have a link to download the master sigils, as well as a pendulum chart for use when communicating with Lilith or any other spirit. I also include directions for crafting your own pendulum.

It is a habit I have now to take a pendulum and small chart with me into the circle. By performing a basic banishment while casting the circle, you can ensure your use of a pendulum will not be adversely affected by negative or misleading energies.

When doing a ritual to obtain answers, make sure you have a pad and pen with you in the circle. It's very possible you will forget the more important information and only recall something trivial.

When working a ritual with the idea of simply meeting Lilith in whatever aspect you choose, be prepared to give her one of the suggested offerings. It's only polite. This is like offering a cup of tea or coffee to a treasured old friend you have invited to your place. (In my case, it's often beer and burnt offerings - AKA barbecue.)

Preparing for the Rituals

Like a lot of the books I write, there isn't a lot of preparation needed for the rituals. Some rituals will refer to a "custom" sigil. I have provided a few, designed to draw money to you, or to bring back someone that you desire to see again.

It's quite easy to craft a custom sigil. There's no weird occult secret to the process. We begin with your petition, or a statement of desire. Look at the statement and make sure it's as simple as possible. Write the statement in the past tense, as if it has already occurred, then link it to Lilith. A good example is below:

"Lilith put me back in touch with (Person's Name)"
Or

"Lilith made sure I got the $— raise"
Keep it very simple. (When writing down money amounts,

spell it out. Write "ONE THOUSAND", versus using numerals, "$1000".)

Next step is to remove the vowels. Such as "A" "E" "I" "O" and "U". Then copy the statement on another line.

"LLTH PT MD SR GT TH (MONEY AMOUNT) RS"

Then remove the extra consonants.

"LTHPMDSRG" - so you have a string of fewer letters. Arrange those into a design.

Such as this sample:

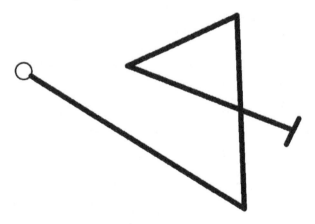

Next, we'll us what is called a gematria to convert letters into numbers. The gematria is the practice of assigning a numerical value to a name, word, or phrase according to an alphanumerical cipher. A single word can yield several values depending on the cipher which is used. Hebrew alphanumeric ciphers were probably used in biblical times and were later adopted by other cultures.

Hebrew doesn't use vowels, so it's perfect to convert the

English alphabet to numbers, and it's the reason why we discard vowels. One can then plot the resulting numbers over a Magick Square of a particular planet. For example, use the planet Venus' square to plot out a sigil for family or love.

Once you have a sigil created, plus any other preparations outlined in each ritual, you can then call on Lilith.

See the examples in the Appendix.

DAVID THOMPSON

PART TWO

THE MAGICK OF THE DAEMONESS

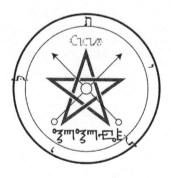

CHAPTER SIX

Ritual for Answers

This is a basic ritual you can do to contact Lilith to gather information about a desire, to get any feedback on a potential ritual, to clarify the results of a previous ritual, or to simply ask questions of Lilith, in her form as a Daemon. This basic ritual can be changed to work for any type of magick you wish to work.

In this type of ritual, it really helps to have a pendulum with you, so you can see her answers being spelled out using a letter pendulum chart. A sample chart is in the appendix, as well as directions on how to use a pendulum in a ritual.

And yes, it is customary to give her an offering with this type of ritual.

Items needed:

Lilith's candles

Daemoness Sigil

Pendulum & pendulum chart(s)

Pad of paper, pen or pencil

Incense

Offering

    If offering a blood sacrifice, a second copy of her sigil

    Diabetic Lancet

    Fire-proof container

Offering bowl

Steps:

    Altar candles lit.

    Incense lit

    Lights off

    Cast circle

    Banishment of negative energies

    Invocation to Lilith

    Great Daemon Lilith! Hear me!

    I now call you!

      Renich viasa avage Lillith lirach

      Renich viasa avage Lillith lirach

      Renich viasa avage Lillith lirach

    I wish for your presence in my sacred space.

    Lilith, Goddess of Darkness. Daemoness of Power.

    Lilith, the Daemoness Divine!

    Lilith, who leads forth the hordes of the Abyss, and leads

man to liberation!

Lilith, whose lips are like red roses, whose kiss tastes of wine!

Lilith, fulfiller of all lust, seer of desire. First of all women!

Queen of the Magic!

Grace me with your presence.

Look for the subtle signs that Lilith is nearby.

Pickup your pendulum, and begin to ask questions.

Once the questions have been answered, you pick up the offering, and say:

"Lilith, I humbly offer you this _____ for answering my questions."

Put the offering into the offering bowl, and place this on her sigil, next to the Ritual Candle.

If working a blood sacrifice, prick a finger and place a single drop of blood onto her extra sigil. Then hold this up and say:

"Lilith! I now give to you my essence, in return for your favor!"

Touch the paper to a candle, and allow the paper to burn completely, then stir the ashes to make sure the paper is completely consumed by the fire.

Now close the ritual as follows:

"Lilith, I adore you with all my being. Our work here is

now done. I now say, you may depart, and please come again when I next call upon you!"

The ritual is now finished.

If offering a non-blood sacrifice, allow the items to stay on the altar overnight, then discard outside.

Otherwise, take the ashes outside and scatter them.

CHAPTER SEVEN

Sex Magick

Sexual magick is separate from Love Magick, in that with sex magick, your goal is to get the other person into bed (or anywhere else you wish to engage in sex). If love later occurs, then it results from the chemistry between the two of you. Love magick, on the other hand, draws the other person to you, and cause the deeper emotions to rise, allowing them to fall in love with you.

This is classic Lust versus Love.

We'll start with the lust part.

Basic Sex Magick

Without resorting to the Sex Slave ritual, working sex magick is pretty easy and straightforward. You need very little preparation and can work a ritual before heading out on the town.

This ritual builds up sexual attraction energy in you, and allow to you project an aura of "hotness". Sexual attraction is tied to energy and, somewhat, the chemistry of pheromones. You will need to purchase, or make, "come to me" oil. A recipe is in the appendix for a very effective oil.

Once you work the physical ritual, you can then work only the pathworking version, as your energy system is already "primed" to attract sexual partners.

A word of caution: You will attract people. Your sexual attractiveness will increase tenfold, so you're going to attract people who will not be your type. Play it safe, and use common sense. You may attract someone who will not back-off, so it's best to have someone near you to act as a bodyguard. (I'm speaking from experience on this.) Just as many men head out with the goal of "getting laid" as women, but sometimes men will act irrationally when targeting a woman.

Prepare your petition, and also a sigil. Keep it simple.

A simple petition can be worded as follows: "Lilith, I ask that you greatly enhance my sex appeal, and that I will attract a willing and safe sex partner."

A sigil from that statement will work very well.

Items needed:

Lilith's candles

Daemoness Sigil

Your petition

A custom sigil

Incense

Red candles

"Come to me" Oil

Offering

   If offering a blood sacrifice, a second copy of her sigil

   Diabetic Lancet

   Fire-proof container

Offering bowl

Steps:

Altar candles lit.

Incense lit

Light two or more red candles

Lights off

Cast circle

Banishment of negative energies

Invocation to Lilith

Great Daemon Lilith! Hear me!

I now call you!

   Renich viasa avage Lillith lirach

   Renich viasa avage Lillith lirach

   Renich viasa avage Lillith lirach

I wish your presence in my sacred space.

Lilith, Goddess of Darkness. Daemoness of Power.

Lilith, the Daemoness Divine!

Lilith, who leads forth the hordes of the Abyss, and leads man to liberation!

Lilith, whose lips are like red roses, whose kiss tastes of wine!

Lilith, fulfiller of all lust, seer of desire. First of all women!

Queen of the Magic!

Grace me with your presence.

At this point, look for the subtle signs that Lilith is nearby.

Present your case. Read your petition.

Pick up the sigil, place a small drop of "Come to Me" oil on it.

Pass it through the incense smoke.

"Lilith, I now ask that you enchant this symbol to enhance my sexual attractiveness to others."

Once the sigil is enchanted, you pick up the offering, and say:

"Lilith, I humbly offer you this _____ for attending to my petition."

Put the offering into the offering bowl, and place this on her sigil, next to the Ritual Candle.

If working a blood sacrifice, prick a finger and place a single drop of blood onto her extra sigil. Then hold this up and say:

"Lilith! I now give to you my essence, in return for your

favor!"

Touch the paper to a candle, and allow the paper to burn completely, then stir the ashes to make sure the paper is completely consumed by the fire.

Pause a few minutes, and meditate on your desired outcome. See it happening. Focus on both the images and feelings you have when your desire manifests.

At this time, place your hand over the sigil.

Now say:

"Into this sigil, I now combine my own god/goddess energy with that of your Dark energy. Together, we will alter space and time so that reality now shifts to allow my sex appeal to manifest! So it is written, so it is done!"

Now close the ritual as follows:

"Lilith, I adore you with all my being. Our work here is now done. I now say, you may depart, and please come again when I next call upon you!"

The ritual is now finished.

Allow the offering to remain on her sigil overnight, then place it outside.

If offering a non-blood sacrifice, allow the items to stay on the altar overnight, then discard outside.

Otherwise, take the ashes outside and scatter them.

Going out afterwards, carry the sigil with you, in a pocket or elsewhere, as long as the image is with you all night.

And good luck!

Pathworking Sex Magick

As with the physical ritual, you will need the come to me oil, and the sigil.

Once you are ready, sit and allow yourself to relax.

Imagine a golden glow starting in your heart area.

This glow expands to completely surround your body.

Now, imagine yourself at the edge of a thick forest.

The sun is suddenly covered by thick clouds.

A huge owl glides overhead.

You find yourself on a forest path.

The owl stares at you from a tree branch.

Talk to the owl. The owl represents Lilith.

Explain to her what you wish to manifest. Imagine yourself in a social situation, and see others around you, attracted by your new sex appeal. Go into as much detail as you can.

Send some energy to the owl, giving thanks for assisting you.

Now, imagine Lilith appearing next to the owl.

Hold up the sigil and ask Lilith to enchant the sigil to attract new lovers to you.

In your mind, hold up a white rose, then prick a finger and let a drop of blood fall onto the rose.

Give this rose to Lilith. Tell her how grateful you are.

You now turn around and walk out of the forest, along a path.

As soon as you exit the forest, the ritual is done.

As soon as possible, anoint the sigil with a small drop of "Come to Me" oil.

Sex Slave Ritual

Some might argue that a spell to turn another into your "sex slave" needs to be in "Subjugation Magick", and they have a point. But this belongs in sex magick because the magick is specifically designed to draw someone to you just for sex.

Alright, folks. All credit is due to the ancient book (only if 1970s is ancient) where I found the original sex slave spell. This book also had a long warning, explaining how compelling someone to act against their own best interest can backfire.

And this spell can have unexpected results.

This particular spell requires a lot of pre-ritual work to gather the correct things needed, creating the special ritual sigil and petition.

But, before I get into the specifics of this ritual, let me tell you what occurred when I worked this one, and what the results were.

The original spell invoked Satan and Beelzebub. The original author made the mistake of assuming these were different names for the same daemon, but they're actually two different energies. You also control them, in that you commanded them, binding them to do your work, along with threats if they failed.

The plus side is that this spell works. The downside is it almost works too well, and the two daemons will demand their due. As in making your life miserable if you fail to honor the extended offerings required for this spell.

Let me tell you what happened.

I was 22, still a student in college. I was in my second year working really hard to perfect my photography and filmmaking. I was in my own place, which I used as a studio (as well as living there).

I had originally gotten into glamor and model photography as a way to meet girls (Yeah, I know…) And it worked. There was a new girl in my apartment almost every week. Many would come back. Unfortunately, their minds were *only* on modeling.

After a few months, I grew frustrated.

I was constantly "friend-zoned" well before it was a term.

I recalled a book my mom had checked out from the library when I was younger and I sought that book out again. A basic guide to witchcraft.

In it was a section of sex spells, primarily for men. It used male energy and a male deity to achieve results. I found the book and copied the spell I wanted (ignoring the stern warnings both before and after). This was a spell for making a specific woman a man's sex slave.

It called upon Lucifer, used blood to craft symbols and circles, used the ground to transmit the energy and was the first spell I ever did that called upon a deity.

I had my target, a young woman who looked like a prettier version of actress/singer Linda Ronstadt (I'm *not* kidding, and she was also a ballet dancer from a rich family in Houston).

I gathered up the needed accessories, and I needed a secluded area with a view of the moon. I prepared the parchment (needed a lot of blood to draw symbols). I then headed out to the lake and a park I knew of, where I could get privacy. I performed the ritual, concluded it as written, and went back into town to await the results.

IT BLOODY WORKED.

Within the promised 3 days, she called, and wanted to do another shoot. That evening, we did the shoot, and we stopped the photography for a break. I asked if she minded if I grilled a couple of steaks. As we sat eating, she looked at me in the eye and asked, "Do you ever date your models?"

BINGO

I won't go into details, but we didn't get back to the shoot for a few more hours.

Because of the success of the spell, I'd gotten a bit cocky. I was given another warning when a friend-zoned model showed up and saw the next parchment and the other stuff.

"WFT are you doing?" she demanded.

I explained, and the girl says "You better not try that shit with me."

"How do you know I haven't already?" I grinned.

"I'll pull your dick out by the root," she warned.

But no, the target this time was an Olivia Newton-John

double, only taller and prettier.   It worked, again. This time the model showed up to "help me in the darkroom" and things developed (horrid pun, yeah).

Then, two problems developed:

One, the first model was still under the spell, and kept showing up. She was in a sorority and enlisted her friends to keep an eye on me. I swear I was being followed, and I'd get weird calls during shoots with other models.

Two, the second model was a tad obsessive. And young, being a freshman.

I realized I could not simply cast this spell, have a few days of fun, and expect them to go away. The second model wanted to move in.

The first kept showing up–during other photo shoots and when the second girl was over.

I asked my friend what to do. She got a good laugh, and I had to accept ownership of the situation.

So, I talked to the blonde model and explained her feelings resulted from a spell I put on her.

She also had a good laugh, and didn't believe in magick. Then I explained that, at the age of 22, I was not at all ready to settle down. Tough. She spent the night.

I went to talk with the first model. She laughed as well. She then told me we were perfect for each other and I had to meet with her father, who was visiting.

Thankfully, her father disapproved of me. Long hair, Hawaiian shirts, my "art".

So, he forbids his daughter from seeing me again.

She, of course, redoubled her efforts.

What did I do? I had another friend, a male friend, who showed me a small charm to break the sex magic, but only after I introduced him to the tall blonde. The blonde wound up moving in with HIM! Phew. I felt sorry for the guy. I do have to ponder how well that worked out for either of them.

The brunette? I tried to break the spell. But by then she was in too deep, so I had to accept my responsibility and I didn't want to hurt her, so we spent the rest of the time I was at UT "dating", for lack of a better word. We lost touch when I moved to DFW (Dallas/Ft Worth) after graduating and she went back to Houston.

The take-away?

- One–I don't work love magic at all now. Unless it's a paying client.
- Two–these things work. They absolutely WORK when done right.
- Three–Daemons love a good show. Especially if it teaches a lesson.

This calls for "magick" paper. I have no idea what was meant by this, but I have found expensive stationary to work just as good.

My rewriting of this spell uses only Lilith, because if ANY daemon can cause someone to come to you and be your sex slave, it's Lilith. During a channeling session, Lilith reminded me of this spell, and told me she was one of the original goddess of sex, and she'd be a better fit for this ritual. I agree. I have NOT TESTED this particular ritual, and it uses the same invocations that were used for Lucifer and Beelzebub, just changed a bit. I honestly doubt Lilith would be harmed in any way by calling down on her the angels and light of Heaven, but it's said anyway.

The ritual follows. You've been warned.

Here's what you'll need:

- A small black candle.
- "Magick" paper
- An art quill pen.
- Some ashes (any will do).
- A bit of mineral oil.
- An iron horseshoe.

Preparation:

On the magick paper draw three circles, one inside the other. Like this:

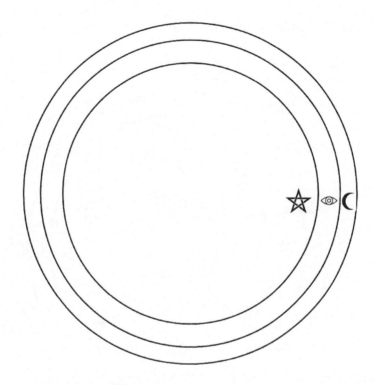

Inside the center, write the woman's name. Use ASHES (any ashes, such as burned paper or ashes from a fire) to write the name with a quill pen. (Mix a bit of oil in the ash to make an ink.)

Now, prick your LEFT THUMB. Use the blood to draw SEVEN pentagrams, POINT UP. Around the circle next to her name.

Draw them equidistant apart.

In the next circle, draw SEVEN open eyes, also equal distances apart.

In the outer circle, draw SEVEN Quarter Moons facing RIGHT.

In the circle, as shown.

Now, fold paper in half, then in half again. Take it, the black candle and iron horseshoe, go to a seclude spot outdoors. FACE north. Place the candle on the ground, kneel before the candle, light it, hold the horseshoe with your LEFT hand, aim it to the moon, and burn the paper as you recite the following:

Renich viasa avage Lillith lirach

[Ren-ich Vee-Ah-Sah Ah-Vage Lilith Lee-rach]

Lilith! Daemoness of the Night, of the Moon, the Stars

All-seeing eye,

HEAR ME!

Renich viasa avage Lillith lirach

[Ren-ich Vee-Ah-Sah Ah-Vage Lilith Lee-rach]

Lilith! I summon you!

Lilith! Thou who tempted Eve with the apple!

All of the fallen angels of the realm,

Hear Me!

I command that you come here to this place

And Listen To Me!

Get this woman (her name)

And bring her to me!

Drive her to me!

Take her soul and give it to me!

Goddess of the Night, Great Daemon Lilith!

Do as I command

Or I will curse you with angels

And the Eternal Light of Heaven.

When the paper burns out, repeat the incantation. While doing so, draw a cross on your chest, over your heart, with the ashes.

Visualize for a few minutes what you want, the woman, etc.

Snuff out the candle when you have finished the meditation.

Then bury the candle, the ashes and horseshoe where you knelt.

To Return a Lost Lover (Against their will)

Unlike the Return Ritual using the Goddess Lilith, this one will actually drag a lost lover back to you. Once they return, it is up to you to convince them to stick around. Like the previous ritual, this ritual also breaks all the rules when it comes to free-will. The lost person will return. They may not be too happy about it. I'd use this ritual only if the pre-birth soul-contract hasn't been completed, or you need closure.

For this ritual, you will need a photograph of the person, and a piece of their essence, such as hair or nail clippings, to completely tie the magick to their very being.

This ritual is best performed between the new and full moon, on a Tuesday or Saturday, where you will use the baneful energy of those planets.

Create a sigil of the end result, such as "(Their Name) has returned to me." Or use the "Compel Sigil" included in the sigil downloads for this book.

When writing your petition, you can elaborate on that statement. Such as "Powerful Lilith, I ask that you bring (their name) back to me, shackled and chained if necessary. They are to return to me before the moon completes a single cycle. So be it!"

You will be best served by working the full ritual for this, but a pathworking ritual is included.

The Ritual

Items needed:

Lilith's candles

Daemoness Sigil

Your petition

Sigil

Photograph of the target person

Incense

Red candle

Offering

   If offering a blood sacrifice, a second copy of her sigil

   Diabetic Lancet

   Fire-proof container

Offering bowl

Any oils necessary (command oil is best)

Steps:

Light altar candles.

Incense lit

Lights off

Cast circle

Banishment of negative energies

Invocation to Lilith

Great Daemon Lilith! Hear me!

I now call you!

   Renich viasa avage Lillith lirach

   Renich viasa avage Lillith lirach

   Renich viasa avage Lillith lirach

I wish your presence in my sacred space.

Lilith, Goddess of Darkness. Daemoness of Power.

Lilith, the Daemoness Divine!

Lilith, who leads forth the hordes of the Abyss, and leads man to liberation!

Lilith, whose lips are like red roses, whose kiss tastes of wine!

Lilith, fulfiller of all lust, seer of desire. First of all women!

Queen of the Magic!

Grace me with your presence.

At this point, look for the subtle signs that Lilith is near.

Present your case. Read your petition.

Pick up the ritual candle, and hold it up.

"Oh, Lilith, I ask that you now enchant this candle to bring (name) back to me, chained and bound!"

Light the candle and place it on her sigil.

Pick up the sigil you made, and write the person's name on the back. If using a photograph, also write on the back: "(Name) Come Back to Me!"

Turn the sigil over a place a small drop of "Command Oil" onto it.

Pass it through the incense smoke.

"Lilith, I now ask that you enchant this symbol to bring (their name) back to me."

Once the sigil is enchanted, you pick up the offering, and say:

"Lilith, I humbly offer you this _____ for attending to my petition."

Put the offering into the offering bowl, and place this on her sigil, next to the red ritual candle.

If working a blood sacrifice, prick a finger and place a single drop of blood onto her extra sigil. Then hold this up and say:

"Lilith! I now give to you my essence, in return for your favor!"

Touch the paper to a candle, and allow the paper to burn completely, then stir the ashes to make sure the paper is completely consumed by the fire.

Take a minute or two to meditate and visualize the desire manifesting.

Place your hand over the sigil or the petition.

Now say:

"Lilith! I now combine my own god/goddess energy with that of your Dark energy. Together, we will alter space and time so that (name) returns to me quickly and without fail! So it is written, so it is done!"

Now close the ritual as follows:

"Lilith, I adore you with all my being. Our work here is now done. I now say, you may depart, and please come again when I next call upon you!"

The ritual is now finished.

If offering a non-blood sacrifice, allow the items to stay on the altar overnight, then discard outside.

Otherwise, take the ashes outside and scatter them.

Return of a Lover Pathworking

This ritual will draw Lilith to you, and have her track down and drag that person to you. Make sure you won't be disturbed for several minutes, and have the photo of the target with you, as well as the sigil you created.

Once you are ready, sit and allow yourself to relax.

Imagine a golden glow starting in your heart area.

This glow expands to completely surround your body.

Now, imagine yourself at the edge of a thick forest.

The sun is suddenly covered by thick clouds.

A huge owl glides overhead.

You find yourself on a forest path.

The owl stares at you from a tree branch.

Talk to the owl. The owl represents Lilith.

Ask Lilith to help you return this person to your life. Explain why.

In your mind, hold up the photograph to show the owl.

Visualize this person contacting you. Run a mental movie where this happens.

Send some energy to the owl, giving thanks for assisting you.

Pick up your sigil and ask Lilith to appear.

She will now appear near the owl. Hold up the sigil and ask her to activate it, to bring this person to you.

In your mind, hold up a white rose, then prick a finger and let a drop of blood fall onto the rose.

Give this rose to Lilith. Tell her how grateful you are.

You now turn around and walk out of the forest, along a path.

As soon as you exit the forest, the ritual is done.

To further thank Lilith, as soon as you can, print her sigil, prick your finger and drop some blood onto her sigil. Burn the sigil, and take the ashes outside and release them into the wind.

CHAPTER EIGHT

Protection Magick

This type of magick uses Lilith in her Daemoness form, which can generate a better shield than a goddess.

There's not a lot you need for this ritual, except for a special sigil for the protection. This ritual can be worked for yourself or for someone else. If working for a friend, get a recent photo of them to use in the ritual.

The petition will be worded differently with each circumstance. I have a general protection sigil for this and the other protection rituals.

To protect yourself, word your petition as follows:

"Lilith! I ask that you use your powers to place an impenetrable shield around me, to protect me from all attacks, physical and energetic."

To protect others, obtain a photograph and use this in the

ritual. Word the petition like this:

"Lilith! I ask that you provide (name) with your powerful energy to protect them from all attacks, both physical and energetic."

Feel free to go into more detail on why the protection is needed.

Items needed:

Lilith's candles

Daemoness Sigil

Your petition

Protection sigil

Photograph (if for someone else)

Incense

Small black ritual candle

Offering

If offering a blood sacrifice, a second copy of her sigil

Diabetic Lancet

Fire-proof container

Offering bowl

Mineral oil and black salt (*see appendix)

Steps:

Light altar candles.

Incense lit

Lights off

Cast circle

Banishment of negative energies

Invocation to Lilith

Great Daemon Lilith! Hear me!

I now call you!

Renich viasa avage Lillith lirach

Renich viasa avage Lillith lirach

Renich viasa avage Lillith lirach

I wish your presence in my sacred space.

Lilith, Goddess of Darkness. Daemoness of Power.

Lilith, the Daemoness Divine!

Lilith, who leads forth the hordes of the Abyss, and leads man to liberation!

Lilith, whose lips are like red roses, whose kiss tastes of wine!

Lilith, fulfiller of all lust, seer of desire. First of all women!

Queen of the Magic!

Grace me with your presence.

At this point, look for the subtle signs that Lilith is near.

Present your case. Read your petition.

Pick up the black ritual candle, and hold it up.

"Oh, Lilith, I ask that you now enchant this candle to protect (me) or (name)."

Lightly coat the candle with oil, then dust the black salt on it.

Place the candle in a good holder.

Light the candle and place it on her sigil.

Take the protection sigil and hold it up now.

Pass it through the incense smoke.

"Lilith, I now ask that you enchant this symbol to protect (me) or (name)."

Once the sigil is enchanted, you pick up the offering, and say:

"Lilith, I humbly offer you this _____ for attending to my petition."

Put the offering into the offering bowl, and place this on her sigil, next to the Ritual Candle.

If working a blood sacrifice, prick a finger and place a single drop of blood onto her extra sigil. Then hold this up and say:

"Lilith! I now give to you my essence, in return for your favor!"

Touch the paper to a candle, and allow the paper to burn completely, then stir the ashes to make sure the paper is completely consumed by the fire.

Take a minute or two to meditate and visualize the desire manifesting.

At this time, place your hand over the sigil or the petition. Now say:

"Into this sigil and petition, I now combine my own energy with that of your Dark energy. Together, we will alter space and time so that reality now shifts to allow to shield (me) or (name)! So it is written, so it is done!"

Now close the ritual as follows:

"Lilith, I adore you with all my being. Our work here is now done. I now say, you may depart, and please come again when I next call upon you!"

The ritual is now finished.

Allow the offering to remain on her sigil overnight, then place it outside.

If offering a non-blood sacrifice, allow the items to stay on the altar overnight, then discard outside.

Otherwise, take the ashes outside and scatter them.

Pathworking Protection

For this version, you will need the Protection Sigil, and a photo of who you want to extend Lilith's protective shield over, if this is for someone else.

We'll be contacting Lilith in her form as a Daemoness, starting with the established pathworking I developed for an earlier book, then going a bit further.

Get comfortable and allow yourself to go into Alpha.

When ready, visualize the following as vividly as you possibly can.

Once you are ready, sit and allow yourself to relax.

Imagine a golden glow starting in your heart area.

This glow expands to completely surround your body.

Now, image that you are in a beautiful garden of flowers. Roses and lilies.

Now, you are at the edge of a quiet pond with a single swan.

There is a fresh breeze in your face.

A path at your feet, you follow it.

You are led into a walled garden. Sturdy rock walls surround you.

A woman walks towards you, Lilith.

She is in a red dress.

On her shoulder is an Owl.

Greet Lilith.

Explain to her what is needed. Hold the sigil and, if needed, the photo of the friend.

Lilith may nod, acknowledging your request.

Visualize the following now:

Lilith lifts her arms, and a bright silver light erupts from her hands. This light surrounds you (or the person in the photo).

The shielding solidifies, becoming as hard as armor. Lilith releases the owl, and it flies in a circle above you, keeping watch.

Thank Lilith by projecting to her pink energy. This energy flows from your heart center and into her heart center.

Now visualize the protection sigil glowing with a silver light. Watch it glow and watch the silver become brighter and brighter.

In your mind, now visualize turning and walking away from the garden, still surrounded by the silver armor.

This ritual is now complete. Open your eyes.

Keep her sigil with you, in a wallet, purse, or keep near you.

If this is for a friend, give the sigil to them.

Mess 'Em Up

Another type of protection magick is to not only protect you, but to send that harmful energy right back at the person sending it. I always say, "Turnabout is fair play."

This one uses Pathworking, plus a protection sigil. It can be easily combined with the other protection ritual, by simply meditating on the issue and visualizing the energy being reflected from the silver armor and back at the other magician.

In 2003, I became entangled with someone who needed some straightening out, so to speak. My father was doing remodeling work for this woman who, among other things, claimed to be a channel for an Indian Guru. She insisted he bring me over to meet her. First things, she decided to "read me" and told me I had a curse on me. Then she put her hand on my head and said she was removing this curse. Her hand grew quite cold. (Clue number one that something was wrong.) Before meeting her, I was becoming frustrated in "manifesting". It seemed as if nothing was working. This woman told me that my "karmic path" is wrong, and I had to give up my business and move in a different direction, and that I had all this bad karma.

Skip forward a few weeks, and still nothing was improving. It was spiraling out of control. This woman kept wanting me to sell everything, give up my daughter to the kid's mom, and all this other stuff. Somehow, against my usual better judgment, I was falling for this. Then I had a weird dream, where this little bald guy and I were playing golf. He tells me, "Never worship a god outside of yourself, and to get your ass away from that woman."

The next day, I get a message on a social group place called "Delphi", from a young lady with a message for me. She tells me in private chat she has this old guy (from my dream) needing to talk to me, that he is her guide. He is also sometimes my guide, and the message was vitally important.

Since this young woman was close by, we met up. When we met, I got hit by the (now very usual) sensations that I knew her already. We talked for quite a while. The guide's message to me was to get rid of that "guru woman", as she was doing her best to siphon my energy, and had been doing it for quite a while.

I was also introduced to my "soul father", a guide named Daniel. The bald old man who played golf with me.

So, I tell the crazy guru lady to go away. She loses it. I start getting hit by serious energy. I contacted the young woman again, and she reminded me I should work "good, old-fashioned magick" on the situation, and that a specific goddess wanted to help.

Thinking about all that, I headed to a local grocery store. I spotted that guru woman in the store, and she kept avoided me, but stared at me. At the checkout, my debit card wouldn't work.

I had to pay with a paper check. I caught this woman staring at me, and I knew why the card didn't work. Alright, enough was enough.

It was that very night I worked a ritual to Lilith.

I was guided by Lilith this time to counterattack this "guru woman", which involved a lot of visuals.

For this pathworking ritual, I'll give you what I was shown to do.

Turnabout is fair play.

This pathworking appears to be quite complicated, but it's actually simple, once you practice the visuals a few times. Work a small section at a time, referring to the instructions, until you are very familiar with the steps.

You do not have to know who is attacking you. You can ask Lilith to direct the reflection back to the source. That is sufficient.

Know what you need to have done, and have the protection sigil with you.

Get comfortable and allow yourself to relax, and go into Alpha.

When ready, visualize the following as vividly as you possibly can.

Once you are ready, sit and allow yourself to relax.

Imagine a golden glow starting in your heart area.

This glow expands to completely surround your body.

Now, imagine you are in a beautiful garden of flowers.

Roses and lilies.

Now, you are at the edge of a quiet pond with a single swan.

There is a fresh breeze in your face.

A path at your feet, you follow it.

You are led into a walled garden. Sturdy rock walls surround you.

A woman walks towards you, Lilith.

She is in a red dress.

On her shoulder is an Owl.

Greet Lilith.

Express to her what is going on and how you wish to handle it.

Take a minute to visualize the following:

A golden shield of energy surrounds you.

It becomes a swirling cloud of energy, whipping all around you.

See now the energy that is attacking you.

Lilith enters the swirling gold energy,

She holds up her hands, which now direct the attacking energy away.

Visualize this attacking energy seeking out the source.

Imagine that energy now engulfing the person sending it.

As they send more energy, more energy is reflected onto them.

The energy now sends orbs of light flying.

Increase this energy that is hitting them.

As suddenly as it started, it now stops.

(Lilith may turn to you, dusting off her hands, as if to say: "Done!")

Ask Lilith, by projecting the thought, to remove that person's ability to ever work magick again.

Hold up the protection sigil. Ask Lilith to energize it.

After this is done, thank Lilith by projecting pink energy towards her.

You now turn and walk along the path away from the garden.

The ritual is now complete. When you can, work an offering to Lilith in the form of either your blood on her sigil, burnt meat, or a raw egg.

CHAPTER NINE

Revenge

Revenge.

When I was a kid, there was a comedy album (from a now disgraced comic) that I listened to over and over. The best track was "Revenge". Here, the guy waited months to get a kid back for hitting him with a slushy snow ball. So, he made the perfect snowball to get the kid back. And waited. And waited. The kid never went outside, so he had to put the "perfect slushball" into the freezer. After spending the next few months being friendly with this other kid, in July he finally had his chance, and went to get the snowball from the freezer, and it had been thrown away.

So, sometimes revenge doesn't actually happen the way you want it to happen. That's why we have magick and curses!

I once asked an online group about revenge. Is it a curse or is it standard magick? Once the flames calmed down, the consensus of anyone left talking to me seemed to point towards "curse". I had to wade through remark after remark about how one should allow "Karma" to deal with the offending person. I felt that sometimes we have to help Mama Karma in her tasks of dealing with those who, in one way or another, deserve a good curse for being a nasty person. It's a good idea to help speed up the process.

A basic revenge ritual can be worked for yourself or another person. Think about what should happen, and ponder this for a while. Or you can just unleash Lilith to take care of it.

The petition for a revenge curse should be well thought out, and leave nothing to chance. Try to give clear directions to Lilith. When creating a sigil for this, try to reduce the statement to as few of words as possible.

A good statement would be: "I ask that Lilith please deal with _____ for the harm they have done to me (or the victim)." It still may make a complicated sigil, but it's needed.

Black salt is used on the black candle as a way to prevent any rebounding of this magick. Place the black candle into a sturdy holder, as it needs to be on the sigil and must burn completely down. Avoid drafts and make sure there is no contact between the flame and the sigil.

We'll be calling on Lilith in her Daemoness aspect for this.

Items needed:

Lilith's candles

Daemoness Sigil

Your petition

Revenge Sigil (if you made one)

Incense

Black ritual candle

Black salt

Offering

   If offering a blood sacrifice, a second copy of her sigil

   Diabetic Lancet

   Fire-proof container

Offering bowl

Any oils necessary

Steps:

Light altar candles.

Incense lit

Lights off

Cast circle

Banishment of negative energies

Invocation to Lilith

Great Daemon Lilith! Hear me!

I now call you!

  Renich viasa avage Lillith lirach

  Renich viasa avage Lillith lirach

  Renich viasa avage Lillith lirach

I wish your presence in my sacred space.

Lilith, Goddess of Darkness. Daemoness of Power.

Lilith, the Daemoness Divine!

Lilith, who leads forth the hordes of the Abyss, and leads man to liberation!

Lilith, whose lips are like red roses, whose kiss tastes of wine!

Lilith, fulfiller of all lust, seer of desire. First of all women!

Queen of the Magic!

Grace me with your presence.

At this point, look for the subtle signs that Lilith is near.

Present your case. Read your petition.

Pick up the ritual candle, and hold it up.

"Oh, Lilith, I ask that you now enchant this candle to bring down your mighty wrath upon (name)!"

Coat the candle in some oil, then sprinkle black salt on it.

Light the candle and place it on her sigil.

If you have a dedicated sigil for this desire, hold it up now.

Pass it through the incense smoke.

"Lilith, I now ask that you enchant this symbol to bring about the revenge I demand."

Once the sigil is enchanted, you pick up the offering, and say:

"Lilith, I humbly offer you this _____ for attending to my petition."

Put the offering into the offering bowl, and place this on her sigil, next to the Ritual Candle.

If working a blood sacrifice, prick a finger and place a single drop of blood onto her extra sigil. Then hold this up and say:

"Lilith! I now give to you my essence, in return for your favor!"

Touch the paper to a candle, and allow the paper to burn completely, then stir the ashes to make sure the paper is completely consumed by the fire.

Take a minute or two to meditate and visualize the desire manifesting.

At this time, place your hand over the sigil or the petition.

Now say:

"Into this petition I now combine my own god/goddess energy with that of your Dark energy. Together, we will alter space and time so that reality now shifts to allow this desire to manifest! So it is written, so it is done!"

Now close the ritual as follows:

"Lilith, I adore you with all my being. Our work here is now done. I now say, you may depart, and please come again when I next call upon you!"

The ritual is now finished.

Allow the offering to remain on her sigil overnight, then place it outside.

If offering a non-blood sacrifice, allow the items to stay on the altar overnight, then discard outside.

Otherwise, take the ashes outside and scatter them.

Retribution

This ritual will work for either yourself, or getting retribution for another.

This differs from the basic Revenge Curse in that you are asking Lilith to unmask the offending person and allow the authorities deal with them. This takes some energy, as you are working to see to it that the target comes to the attention of local police and the justice system, or some other authority.

As with the Revenge ritual, you need to clearly spell out in a petition who the person is, and why they deserve to have the police examine them. I suggest this: "Lilith, I come to you now to ask that (their name) be forced to face the consequences for their actions (describe what they did). I ask that they be discovered before any more people are harmed. I ask that you do this quickly!"

Black salt is used on the black candle as a way to prevent any rebounding of this magick. Place the black candle into a sturdy holder, as it needs to be on the sigil and must burn completely down. Avoid drafts and make sure there is no contact between the flame and the sigil.

Items needed:

Lilith's candles

Daemoness Sigil

Your petition

Incense

Black ritual candle

Black salt

Offering

    If offering a blood sacrifice, a second copy of her sigil

    Diabetic Lancet

    Fire-proof container

Offering bowl

Any oils necessary

Steps:

Light altar candles.

Incense lit

Lights off

Cast circle

Banishment of negative energies

Invocation to Lilith

Great Daemon Lilith! Hear me!

I now call you!

    Renich viasa avage Lillith lirach

    Renich viasa avage Lillith lirach

    Renich viasa avage Lillith lirach

I wish your presence in my sacred space.

Lilith, Goddess of Darkness. Daemoness of Power.

Lilith, the Daemoness Divine!

Lilith, who leads forth the hordes of the Abyss, and leads man to liberation!

Lilith, whose lips are like red roses, whose kiss tastes of wine!

Lilith, fulfiller of all lust, seer of desire. First of all women!

Queen of the Magic!

Grace me with your presence.

At this point, look for the subtle signs that Lilith is near.

Present your case. Read your petition.

Pick up the ritual candle and coat it in some oil, then sprinkle black salt on it.

Then hold the candle up.

"Oh, Lilith, I ask that you now enchant this candle to unmask and make public the sins of (name). Bringing about his/her downfall!"

Light the candle and place it on her sigil.

If you have a dedicated sigil for this desire, hold it up now.

Pass it through the incense smoke.

"Lilith, I now ask that you enchant this symbol to bring about the downfall of (name)."

Once the sigil is enchanted, you pick up the offering, and say:

"Lilith, I humbly offer you this _____ for attending to my petition."

Put the offering into the offering bowl, and place this on her sigil, next to the Ritual Candle.

If working a blood sacrifice, prick a finger and place a single drop of blood onto her extra sigil. Then hold this up and say:

"Lilith! I now give over to you my essence, in return for your favor!"

Touch the paper to a candle, and allow the paper to burn completely, then stir the ashes to make sure the paper is completely consumed by the fire.

Take a minute or two to meditate and visualize the desire manifesting.

Place your hand over the sigil or the petition.

Now say:

"Into this petition and sigil I now combine my own god/goddess energy with that of your Dark energy. Together, we will alter space and time so that reality now shifts to allow this desire to manifest! So it is written, so it is done!"

Now close the ritual as follows:

"Lilith, I adore you with all my being. Our work here is now done. I now say, you may depart, and please come again when I next call upon you!"

The ritual is now finished.

Allow the offering to remain on her sigil overnight, then place it outside.

If offering a non-blood sacrifice, allow the items to stay on the altar overnight, then discard outside.

Otherwise, take the ashes outside and scatter them.

CHAPTER TEN

Cursing

Many of the writings about Lilith present rituals for cursing others. I'm including this chapter because I have found Lilith to be quite effective in cursing someone with ill luck and general torment. The target will have to deserve anything you aim at them, so be prepared to tell Lilith *why* you want this person cursed.

A good curse is usually aimed at someone in power, someone who is almost above the law, and out of reach for the usual legal remedies. Perhaps, it is someone like a supervisor at your job, a lawyer or judge who is malevolent, and acts maliciously towards you, or anyone else. Someone who deserves a good, old-fashioned curse. They also should have done something to you, something worth the use of the energy involved in a good curse.

The first step after determining your target is to determine what is needed. Does the target need to suffer public humiliation? Do they need to lose their livelihood? All types of scenarios come to mind: A supervisor suddenly being fired comes to mind, a holier-than-thou neighbor being kicked out of his relationship for cheating, public humiliation, and the ever-popular generational curse against someone who might sabotage your business.

Both rituals need a black candle as the "Ritual" candle. Black salt is used on the candle as a way to prevent any rebounding of this magick. Place this black candle into a sturdy holder, as it needs to be on the sigil and must burn completely down. Avoid drafts and make sure there is no contact between the flame and the sigil.

Due to the topic of these rituals, I was advised not to include pathworking, as this magick really only works when you collect all the needed items, craft a sigil, and do the traditional summoning of Lilith.

Some of the following rituals ask only for a blood offering. Especially when working a curse. Lilith figures if you're not willing to prick a finger for a drop of blood, then is the curse really worth the time in ritual?

Curses! Curses!

Curses are everywhere. Ancient Egyptian curses, "Death Shall Come on Swift Wings to Him Who Disturbs the Peace of the King." Curses cast prior to an execution. The "Curse of the Hope Diamond."

Lilith is the Queen of Curses. Calling on her to cause ill fortune on rivals, nasty neighbors, and other deserving people is the whole idea behind this chapter.

Think long and hard before cursing someone. They really have to deserve it, as curse energy could backfire. Sometimes it's an effect of your own guilt, but often it's Lilith taking a look at the situation and deciding that YOU are the one deserving of the ill fortune, not the target.

In preparation, you will need a photograph of the target, preferably an item of their clothing or sample of their handwriting. When asked by a client to deal with an ex-spouse, I was sent a sock of theirs and their signature from an old letter. This way, the magick is intimately tied to the target.

One ingenious curse was to have the person suddenly suffer from uncontrollable bowel movements during business meetings. I understand this worked very well.

Get creative in the events that can befall the target. Never finding parking. Losing their job. Rashes. Venereal disease. Just don't ask for severe injury or death, unless their crime against you truly deserves it. My daughter was a passenger in a horrendous car crash. Because of that driver's drinking, I cursed that man the evening I learned of the accident. Last time I heard, he was homeless, divorced, and being well punished by Lilith for this stupidity. Yes, I wanted to have him really suffer. But not die. Death is not a punishment. Prolonging a horrible life IS punishment.

The basic petition template is simple: "Lilith, I ask that you curse (name). I ask that (he/she) is cursed will ill-fortune. That (go into details here)."

A Basic Curse

Items needed:

Black altar candles with Lilith's Sigil

Daemoness Sigil

Your petition

Photograph or other items for the target

Incense

Black ritual candle

Black salt

Blood Offering

A second copy of her sigil

Diabetic Lancet

Fire-proof container

Command Oil

Steps:

Light altar candles.

Incense lit

Lights off

Cast circle

Banishment of negative energies

Invocation to Lilith

Great Daemon Lilith! Hear me!

I now call you!

Renich viasa avage Lillith lirach

Renich viasa avage Lillith lirach

Renich viasa avage Lillith lirach

I wish your presence in my sacred space.

Lilith, Goddess of Darkness. Daemoness of Power.

Lilith, the Daemoness Divine!

Lilith, who leads forth the hordes of the Abyss, and leads man to liberation!

Lilith, whose lips are like red roses, whose kiss tastes of wine!

Lilith, fulfiller of all lust, seer of desire. First of all women!

Queen of the Magic!

Grace me with your presence.

At this point, look for the subtle signs that Lilith is near.

Present your case. Read your petition. Explain WHY this person needs to be cursed.

Pick up the ritual candle, and coat it with Command Oil, then sprinkle black salt on it.

"Oh, Lilith, I ask that you now enchant this candle to curse (name) with (go into detail)." Describing your desire.

Light the candle and place it on her sigil.

Now, work the blood sacrifice, prick a finger and place a single drop of blood onto her extra sigil. Then hold this up and say:

"Lilith! I now give to you my essence, in return for your favor!"

Touch the paper to a candle, and allow the paper to burn completely, then stir the ashes to make sure the paper is completely consumed by the fire.

Pause a few minutes, and meditate on your desired outcome. See it happening. Focus on both the images and feelings you have when the target gets hit by the curse.

Take a minute or two to meditate and visualize the desire manifesting.

At this time, place your hand over the sigil or the petition.

Now say:

"Into this curse, I now combine my own god/goddess energy with that of your Dark energy. Together, we will alter space and time so that reality now shifts to allow this desire to manifest! So it is written, so it is done!"

Now close the ritual as follows:

"Lilith, I adore you with all my being. Our work here is now done. I now say, you may depart, and please come again when I next call upon you!"

The ritual is now finished.

Take the ashes from the blood sacrifice outside and scatter them.

Destroying a Business Rival

I have personally used this one. A mediocre competitor was very jealous of my success, and he kept trying to find ways to either use my name to assist him in getting models, claiming to know me, or using copies of my help-wanted notices. He'd submit models to websites, using my name as a reference. His quality was well under par, and I kept hearing he was being rejected. I had an art director call me to ask about this guy. A famous magazine's photo editor called me, saying someone was using my business cards supplied by the magazine to recruit models. Sure enough, a model was tasked by this guy to steal almost half a box of the cards.

I'd finally had enough, and I asked a friend for guidance. She was into doing work as a shaman, and she told me I already knew who to ask for help: Lilith.

So I went into a ritual to neutralize this guy.

As an example of a good petition, we'll use the one I used:

"Lilith, I ask that you assist me in dealing with this person, (name). They persist in (what they're doing). I now ask that you prevent them from (actions) and that you do to them what they wish to do to my business. Prevent them from seeing any success. Prevent them from seeing any profit."

Or words to that effect.

The Ritual

Items needed:

Lilith's candles (both RED)

Daemoness Sigil

Your petition

(Sigil for the desire - optional)

Incense

Black ritual candle

Black salt

Offering

   If offering a blood sacrifice, a second copy of her sigil

   Diabetic Lancet

   Fire-proof container

Offering bowl

Any oils necessary

Steps:

Light altar candles.

Incense lit

Lights off

Cast circle

Banishment of negative energies

Invocation to Lilith

Great Daemon Lilith! Hear me!

I now call you!

   Renich viasa avage Lillith lirach

   Renich viasa avage Lillith lirach

   Renich viasa avage Lillith lirach

I wish your presence in my sacred space.

Lilith, Goddess of Darkness. Daemoness of Power.

Lilith, the Daemoness Divine!

Lilith, who leads forth the hordes of the Abyss, and leads man to liberation!

Lilith, whose lips are like red roses, whose kiss tastes of wine!

Lilith, fulfiller of all lust, seer of desire. First of all women!

Queen of the Magic!

Grace me with your presence.

At this point, look for the subtle signs that Lilith is near.

Present your case. Read your petition.

Pick up the ritual candle and coat it in some oil, then sprinkle black salt on it.

Then hold the candle up.

"Oh, Lilith, I ask that you now enchant this candle to bring about the failure of (name)." and describe your desire.

Light the candle and place it on her sigil.

If you have a dedicated sigil for this desire, hold it up now.

Pass it through the incense smoke.

"Lilith, I now ask that you enchant this symbol to cause (name) to fail utterly."

Once the sigil is enchanted, you pick up the offering, and say:

"Lilith, I humbly offer you this _____ for attending to

my petition."

Put the offering into the offering bowl, and place this on her sigil, next to the Ritual Candle.

If working a blood sacrifice, prick a finger and place a single drop of blood onto her extra sigil. Then hold this up and say:

"*Lilith! I now give to you my essence, in return for your favor!*"

Touch the paper to a candle, and allow the paper to burn completely, then stir the ashes to make sure the paper is completely consumed by the fire.

Take a minute or two to meditate and visualize the desire manifesting.

At this time, place your hand over the sigil or the petition. Now say:

"*Into this sigil and petition, I now combine my own god/goddess energy with that of your Dark energy. Together, we will alter space and time so that reality now shifts to allow this desire to manifest! So it is written, so it is done!*"

Now close the ritual as follows:

"*Lilith, I adore you with all my being. Our work here is now done. I now say, you may depart, and please come again when I next call upon you!*"

The ritual is now finished.

Allow the offering to remain on her sigil overnight, then place it outside.

If offering a non-blood sacrifice, allow the items to stay on the altar overnight, then discard outside.

Otherwise, take the ashes outside and scatter them.

Destroy a Relationship

Occasionally, you may need to sabotage a relationship. My only advice for you, on this subject, is to make sure this is done in the best interest for everyone. Blow-back is almost a certainty if you do this ritual if you are simply wanting your own relationship with one of the people in the relationship, or the relationship you are targeting is healthy and that you simply don't like one of them.

I developed this ritual for a client whose daughter was dating a rough and abusive man. Not only was this guy much older, he was very possessive and jealous, and the man's daughter would return home with suspicious bruises on her arms.

I went into ritual and summoned Lilith into my space. Once I had explained what was needed and why, Lilith was all ready to take care of this man. My client replied that the man was stopped while speeding, then arrested for driving while intoxicated, and while this was happening, the young woman was found in the backseat, with a bruised face. Not only were charges filed against the man, the relationship was destroyed.

Preparation for this ritual includes getting a photograph of the target and drawing a sigil for the end result.

Petition should be worked something like: "Lilith, (name)

is in a toxic relationship, a relationship that will bring (name) harm. I ask that you permanently separate these people without either being harmed."

The sigil's statement can be something like: "(Name) and (Name) are no longer together, and (name) is now safe".

Again, a black candle is used, covered in black salt.

Physical Ritual

Items needed:
> Lilith's black candles
>
> Daemoness Sigil
>
> Your petition
>
> Break-up Sigil
>
> Incense
>
> Black ritual candle
>
> Black salt
>
> Blood offering
>
> Diabetic Lancet
>
> Fire-proof container
>
> Command Oil

Steps:
> Light altar candles.
>
> Incense lit
>
> Lights off
>
> Cast circle

Banishment of negative energies

Invocation to Lilith

Great Daemon Lilith! Hear me!

I now call you!

   Renich viasa avage Lillith lirach

   Renich viasa avage Lillith lirach

   Renich viasa avage Lillith lirach

I wish your presence in my sacred space.

Lilith, Goddess of Darkness. Daemoness of Power.

Lilith, the Daemoness Divine!

Lilith, who leads forth the hordes of the Abyss, and leads man to liberation!

Lilith, whose lips are like red roses, whose kiss tastes of wine!

Lilith, fulfiller of all lust, seer of desire. First of all women!

Queen of the Magic!

Grace me with your presence.

At this point, look for the subtle signs that Lilith is near.

Present your case. Read your petition.

Pick up the ritual candle, and rub some oil on it, then sprinkle the black salt on it.

Hold the candle up, and say:

"Oh, Lilith, I ask that you now enchant this candle to break up (name and name)."

Light the candle and place it on her sigil.

If you have a dedicated sigil for this desire, hold it up now. Pass it through the incense smoke.

"Lilith, I now ask that you enchant this symbol to break up (name and name)."

Once the sigil is enchanted, prick a finger and place a single drop of blood onto her extra sigil.

Then hold this up and say:

"Lilith! I now give to you my essence, in return for your favor!"

Touch the paper to a candle, and allow the paper to burn completely, then stir the ashes to make sure the paper is completely consumed by the fire.

Take a minute or two to meditate and visualize the desire manifesting.

Place your hand over the sigil or the petition.

Now say:

"Into this symbol and petition, I now combine my own god/goddess energy with that of your Dark energy. Together, we will alter space and time so that reality now shifts to allow this desire to manifest! So it is written, so it is done!"

Now close the ritual as follows:

"Lilith, I adore you with all my being. Our work here is now done. I now say, you may depart, and please come again when I next call upon you!"

The ritual is now finished.

Allow the offering to remain on her sigil overnight, then

place it outside.

Take the ashes from the offering outside and scatter them.

CHAPTER ELEVEN

New Money Channels

In her Daemon aspect, Lilith can help open up new channels for income. This can occur as an unexpected windfall (gambling, unexpected tax refund) or when a new opportunity opens up for a better-paying job.

This ritual will use the Lilith Money Draw sigil, found in the appendix.

Word your petition like this: "Lilith, I ask now that you open up new channels for money to flow into my life. I ask that these channels open swiftly, and money flows to me from expected and unexpected sources."

Items needed for the physical ritual:

Lilith's black and red candles

Daemoness Sigil

Your petition

Money Draw Sigil

Incense

A gold or silver ritual candle (green if you can't get the gold or silver)

Offering

    If offering a blood sacrifice, a second copy of her sigil

    Diabetic Lancet

    Fire-proof container

Offering bowl

Crown of Success Oil or Money Draw Oil

Steps:

Altar candles lit.

Incense lit

Lights off

Cast circle

Banishment of negative energies

Invocation to Lilith

Great Daemon Lilith! Hear me!

I now call you!

    Renich viasa avage Lillith lirach

    Renich viasa avage Lillith lirach

    Renich viasa avage Lillith lirach

I wish your presence in my sacred space.

Lilith, Goddess of Darkness. Daemoness of Power.

Lilith, the Daemoness Divine!

Lilith, who leads forth the hordes of the Abyss, and leads man to liberation!

Lilith, whose lips are like red roses, whose kiss tastes of wine!

Lilith, fulfiller of all lust, seer of desire. First of all women!

Queen of the Magic!

Grace me with your presence.

At this point, look for those subtle signals that Lilith is near.

Present your case. Read your petition.

Pick up the ritual candle, and hold it up.

"Oh, Lilith, I ask that you now enchant this candle open up money channels to me, allowing money to flow to me."

Light the candle and place it on her sigil.

If you have a dedicated sigil for this desire, hold it up now.

Pass it through the incense smoke.

"Lilith, I now ask that you enchant this symbol to bring about the money I desire."

Once the sigil is enchanted, you pick up the offering, and say:

"Lilith, I humbly offer you this _____ for attending to my petition."

Put the offering into the offering bowl, and place this on her sigil, next to the Ritual Candle.

If working a blood sacrifice, prick a finger and place a single drop of blood onto her extra sigil. Then hold this up and say:

"Lilith! I now give to you my essence, in return for your favor!"

Touch the paper to a candle, and allow the paper to burn completely, then stir the ashes to make sure the paper is completely consumed by the fire.

Pause a few minutes, and meditate on your desired outcome. See it happening. Focus on both the images and feelings you have when your desire manifests.

Place your hand over the sigil or the petition.

Now say:

"Into this petition, I now combine my own god/goddess energy with that of your Dark energy. Together, we will alter space and time so that reality now shifts to allow new money channels to manifest! So it is written, so it is done!"

Now close the ritual as follows:

"Lilith, I adore you with all my being. Our work here is now done. I now say, you may depart, and please come again when I next call upon you!"

The ritual is now finished.

Allow the offering to remain on her sigil overnight, then place it outside.

If offering a non-blood sacrifice, allow the items to stay on the altar overnight, then discard outside.

Otherwise, take the ashes outside and scatter them.

Pathworking Open New Money Channel Ritual

Once you are ready, sit and allow yourself to relax. Go into Alpha.

Imagine a golden glow starting in your heart area.

This glow expands to completely surround your body.

Now, imagine yourself at the edge of a thick forest.

The sun is suddenly covered by thick clouds.

A huge owl glides overhead.

You find yourself on a forest path.

The owl stares at you from a tree branch.

Talk to the owl. The owl represents Lilith.

State your desire. Go into detail.

Visualize the results. Take your time with this.

Next, send some energy to the owl, giving thanks for assisting you.

Pick up the Money Draw sigil and ask Lilith to appear.

She will now appear near the owl. Hold up the sigil and ask her to activate it, to bring new opportunities for money to flow to you.

Again, visualize the new money channels opening up.

See, as vividly as possible, stacks of money flowing towards you.

Sit with this vision for as long as you desire.

Next, in your mind, hold up a white rose, then prick a finger and let a drop of blood fall onto the rose.

Give this rose to Lilith. Tell her how grateful you are.

You now turn around and walk out of the forest, along a path.

As soon as you exit the forest, the ritual is done.

Money Bags Ritual

This is literally what this ritual brings.

Bags of money.

This ritual will use Lilith in her Daemoness aspect. She'll work with you quickly to bring you unexpected income, but she will do it safely.

This ritual relies upon mental visualization, and the petition and desire spoken aloud.

Ritual items needed:

Altar candles, black and red.

Candles for money: Gold, Green, or silver

"Money" incense, usually frankincense with crushed cloves and cinnamon. If using incense stick, pick a decent "Money Draw" incense.

Money Draw oil (see appendix)

Your petition to Lilith

Offerings: Raw egg, a drop of your blood on her sigil, raw red meat.

Props such as photos of stacks of money, plastic coins, toy money bags. (*optional)

The ritual:

Place Lilith's Daemoness Sigil in the center of the altar

Start incense and light altar candles.

Lights out.

Cast the circle.

Summon Lilith.

Great Daemon Lilith! Hear me!

I now call you!

Renich viasa avage Lillith lirach

Renich viasa avage Lillith lirach

Renich viasa avage Lillith lirach

I wish for your presence in my sacred space.

Lilith, Goddess of Darkness. Daemoness of Power.

Lilith, the Daemoness Divine!

Lilith, who leads forth the hordes of the Abyss, and leads man to liberation!

Lilith, whose lips are like red roses, whose kiss tastes of wine!

Lilith, fulfiller of all lust, seer of desire. First of all women!

Queen of the Magic!

Grace me with your presence.

Wait a few moments, watch for the signs she is near.

At this point, pick up your petition, address Lilith, and speak aloud your petition.

"Dear Lilith….

End this petition with a phrase such as *"As it is written so it is done!"*

At this time, pause for a few breaths and visualize the desire occurring. Go into detail and don't worry if you're taking too long. Just visualize.

Pick up the money candle, and place a few drops of oil on it. Use both hands and gently draw the oil onto the candle.

Set the candle into its holder and say:

"Lilith, I now ask you to bless this candle to open for me new money channels and opportunities to draw money into my life!"

Light the candle and place it near the petition.

Once this is done, pick up the offering and hold it up over your altar.

Say the following:

"Lilith! I give my heartfelt thanks to you for appearing and listening to my prayers of request. In gratitude, I humbly offer you this _____"

Place the offering on Lilith's sigil.

At this point, pause and take a few deep breaths.

Hold your hands over the petition and say (as strongly as you can):

"Into this petition and candle, I now project power drawn from Lilith and drawn from me. All that I have asked for shall now manifest for me! So be it!"

It's now time to end the ritual. Do so by using her common dismissal statement:

"Great and Wonderful Lilith! I thank you again for

attending to my prayers. I ask now that you depart with peace and love. And so it is!"

This ritual is now complete. Room lights on, and all but the money draw candle is extinguished.

Allow the offering to stay on the altar overnight, then dispose of it outside.

Daemoness Money Bags Pathworking

This is a mental only ritual. All you need is a few moments of peace and not be disturbed.

If possible, lower the room lights.

Contact the Daemoness Lilith by visualizing:

Imagine a golden glow starting in your heart area.

This glow expands to completely surround your body.

Now, imagine a bright day, clear blue sky above.

Green grass spreads out under your feet.

A clear bubble appears in the blue sky above you.

It drifts closer. And closer.

It turns bright red, solidifying.

Daemoness Lilith appears in the reddish light.

She smiles.

You now say, out loud or in your mind,

"Dear Lilith, I thank you for coming to my aid.

"I ask that this now occur,"

Visualize bags of cash appearing around you.

A large amount of loose cash now flows down and around you.

Now visualize:

She holds up the large gold bubble.

As she lifts the bubble,

Money bursts out of the bubble, flowing at you.

The money drifts and falls all around you, piling up higher and higher.

Daemoness Lilith will hold this up for a few moments, and then she smiles at you.

Thank Lilith by visualizing:

Hold your hands out and form a PINK ball of energy.

The energy of love and gratitude.

Gently send this ball to Lilith and watch it swell and engulf the goddess.

At this time, Lilith will depart. See the following:

Daemoness Lilith fades into the ball of pink energy. The ball drifts up into the blue sky,

And it slowly fades from view.

This ritual is now complete.

Take a few deep breaths and return to your usual activities.

Part Three

Magick of the Goddess Lilith

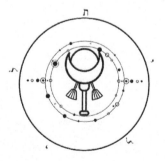

CHAPTER TWELVE

Lilith the Goddess

We now turn away from the dark magick, and to the light. Lilith as a Goddess, full of love, full of warmth, and as gentle as a spring rain.

Sort of.

The major differences between Lilith the Goddess and Lilith the Daemoness is only one of perspective. All beings we use in magick have a dark and a light aspect. In Lilith's case, the line between the two is somewhat blurred. Causing disruption is a dark power. Even retribution is a dark power, because along the way, the target is, if not physically, at least emotionally harmed.

Like her daemon magick, her goddess magick is also the magick of empowerment. With goddess magick, we look at magick that assists you in gaining something: money, power, family, success, and more.

Offerings to the Goddess: We do not work blood offerings to the Goddess Lilith. Instead, offer her flowers, fresh fruit, cream, organic honey, wine, or another spirit.

Ritual for Answers

This is a basic ritual you can do to gather information about a desire, to any feedback on a potential ritual, to clarify the results of a previous ritual, or to simply ask questions of Lilith. This basic ritual can be changed to work for any type of magick you wish to work.

This type of ritual requires you to have a pendulum if possible, so you can see her answers being spelled out using a letter pendulum chart. A sample chart is in the appendix, as well as directions on how to use a pendulum in a ritual.

And yes, it is customary to give her an offering with this type of ritual.

Items needed:
Lilith's candles
Goddess Sigil
Incense
Offering
Offering bowl
Pendulum, pendulum chart and a notepad with pen or pencil

Steps:

Altar candles lit.

Incense lit

Lights off

Cast circle

Banishment of negative energies

Invocation to Goddess Lilith

Goddess Lilith! Hear me!

I invoke you!

For I wish your presence in my sacred space.

Lilith, Goddess of Light. Goddess of Beauty.

Goddess of Empowerment!

Thy whose lips are rose red, whose kiss is as sweet as wine!

Be with me!

You have had many forms throughout time

Grace me with your presence.

At this point, look for subtle the signs that Lilith is near.

Think about your question and meditate for a moment.

Pick up the pendulum and hold it over the letter chart.

Once you are finished asking questions, pick up the offering, and say:

"Goddess Lilith, I humbly offer you this _____ for attending to my prayers."

Put the offering into the offering bowl, and place this on her sigil.

Now close the ritual as follows:

"Goddess Lilith, your energy fills me with your loving grace. I adore you with all my being. Our work here is now done. I now say, you may depart, and please come again when I next call upon you!"

Allow the offering to remain on her sigil overnight. Then discard outside.

CHAPTER THIRTEEN

Success Magick

A ritual for general success to the Goddess Lilith.

Is this for successfully finishing school and a degree? Success with a job application? This ritual can be adjusted to ensure success in most any undertaking.

Candle colors for this will be pink, for pink is a wish-fulfillment color.

Purchase or make Crown of Success oil, and make a copy of the Success sigil.

Ritual items needed:

Lilith's Altar candles

Goddess Sigil

Your petition

Success Sigil

Incense

Ritual candle

Offering

Offering bowl

Crown of Success oil

Steps:

Light altar candles.

Incense lit

Lights off

Cast circle

Banishment of negative energies

Invocation to Goddess Lilith

Goddess Lilith! Hear me!

I invoke you!

For I wish your presence in my sacred space.

Lilith, Goddess of Light. Goddess of Beauty

Goddess of Empowerment!

Thy whose lips are rose red, whose kiss is as sweet as wine!

Be with me!

You have had many forms throughout time

Grace me with your presence.

Look for the subtle signs that Lilith is near.

Present your case. Read your petition.

Pick up the ritual candle, and hold it up.

"Goddess Lilith, I ask that you now enchant this candle to being success to me in whatever enterprise I shall undertake!"

Light the candle and place it on her sigil.

If you have a dedicated sigil for this desire, hold it up now. Pass it through the incense smoke.

"Goddess Lilith, I now ask that you enchant this symbol to bring about the success I desire."

Pause a few minutes, and meditate on your desired outcome. See it happening. Focus on both the images and feelings you have when your desire manifests.

Once the sigil is enchanted, you pick up the offering, and say:

"Goddess Lilith, I humbly offer you this _____ for attending to my prayers."

Put the offering into the offering bowl, and place this on her sigil, next to the Ritual Candle.

At this time, place your hand over the sigil or the petition.

Now say:

"Into this sigil and into this petition, I now combine my own god/goddess energy with that of your Goddess energy. Together, we will alter space and time so that my reality now shifts to allow success to manifest! So it is written, so it is done!"

Now close the ritual as follows:

"Goddess Lilith, your energy fills me with your loving grace. I adore you with all my being. Our work here is now

done. I now say, you may depart, and please come again when I next call upon you!"

Allow the offering to remain on her sigil overnight. Then discard outside.

Pathworking Success Magick

A copy of the success sigil is needed, as well as the petition.

As always, when ready, get comfortable and work the following visuals:

A bright day, clear blue sky above.

Green grass spreads out under your feet.

A clear bubble appears in the blue sky above you.

It drifts closer. And closer.

It turns bright gold, solidifying.

Goddess Lilith appears in the golden light.

She smiles.

You now say, out loud or in your mind, your petition and desire.

Take a minute to fully visualize the desire manifesting. Go into detail!

Now say:

"Goddess, I thank you for coming to my aid. I ask that this now occur,"

Hold that for a few moments, then visualizing PINK light surrounding you.

This PINK light activates the petition and sigil if you made one.

At this point, give thanks to Lilith for assisting you.

Send this pink light to her as an energy offering.

She will now vanish, leaving only an outline.

In your mind, turn around and walk away from the scene.

Open your eyes. Take a few moments to return to fully awakened consciousness.

This ritual is now competed.

Success in Business

This type of magick is useful when just starting a business, and when you have an ongoing business that just needs a boost.

It's separate from the general success ritual because of the subtle differences in how this ritual is worked. You also need gold candles. Gold usually equates wealth, and a successful business will generate wealth.

The key is to define what business success will actually look like. More clients? More sales? Finding investors? You need to reflect on what success means to you before working this magick. For me, success is a sizable balance in the bank, along with enough books lined up to release one every six to eight weeks. When I was doing photography, it was clients booking me months in advance, and plenty of subjects to satisfy each client.

Once you define success, then turn towards writing the petition. A general "Success" sigil is at the end of this book, so just focus on the petition.

I will often phrase a success petition like this: "Lilith! I ask that you assist me in achieving success in my business. That I have plenty of well-paying clients, and they are lining up to hire me."

Items Needed:

Lilith's Altar candles

Goddess Sigil

Your petition

Success Sigil

Incense

Gold or Green ritual candle

Offering

Offering bowl

An item that represents your business, like a card or other item used in your business (in my case, a camera)

Crown of Success Oil

Steps:

Light altar candles.

Incense lit

Lights off

Cast circle

Banishment of negative energies

Invocation to Goddess Lilith

Goddess Lilith! Hear me!

I invoke you!

For I wish your presence in my sacred space.

Lilith, Goddess of Light. Goddess of Beauty.

Goddess of Empowerment!

Thy whose lips are rose red, whose kiss is as sweet as wine!

Be with me!

You have had many forms throughout time

Grace me with your presence.

At this point, look for the subtle signs that Lilith is near.

Present your case. Read your petition.

Pick up the gold ritual candle, place a drop of Crown of Success oil on it,

Then, hold up the candle.

"Goddess Lilith, I ask that you now enchant this candle to quickly bring to me success in my (business)."

Light the candle and place it on her sigil.

Pick up the Success Sigil. Place a single drop of Crown of Success oil on it.

Pass it through the incense smoke.

"Goddess Lilith, I now ask that you enchant this symbol to bring about the success I desire."

Pause a few minutes, and meditate on your desired outcome. See it happening. Focus on the images of when your desire manifests.

Once the sigil is enchanted, you pick up the offering, and say:

"Goddess Lilith, I humbly offer you this _____ for attending to my prayers."

Put the offering into the offering bowl, and place this on her sigil, next to the Ritual Candle.

At this time, place your hand over the sigil or the petition. Now say:

"Into this sigil and petition, I now combine my own god/goddess energy with that of your Goddess energy. Together, we will alter space and time so that my reality now shifts to allow this desire to manifest! So it is written, so it is done!"

You can also charge your business item, card, or brochure, at this same time.

Now close the ritual as follows:

"Goddess Lilith, your energy fills me with your loving grace. I adore you with all my being. Our work here is now done. I now say, you may depart, and please come again when I next call upon you!"

Make sure the Ritual candle can burn harming nothing. All the other candles can be extinguished.

Allow the offering to remain on her sigil overnight. Then discard outside.

Pathworking Business Success

A copy of the success sigil is needed, as well as the petition.

Any props from your business should also be next to you while working this.

As always, when ready, get comfortable and work the following visuals:

A bright day, clear blue sky above.

Green grass spreads out under your feet.

A clear bubble appears in the blue sky above you.

It drifts closer. And closer.

It turns bright gold, solidifying.

Goddess Lilith appears in the golden light.

She smiles.

You now say, out loud or in your mind, your petition and desire.

Take a minute to fully visualize the desire manifesting. Go into detail!

Now say:

"Goddess, I thank you for coming to my aid. I ask that this now occur,"

Hold that for a few moments, then visualizing PINK light surrounding you.

This PINK light activates the petition and sigil if you made one.

At this point, give thanks to Lilith for assisting you.

Send this pink light to her as an energy offering.

She will now vanish, leaving only an outline.

In your mind, turn around and walk away from the scene.

Open your eyes. Take a few moments to return to fully awakened consciousness.

This ritual is now competed.

CHAPTER FOURTEEN

Rituals for Money

I have money rituals for Lilith in her Daemoness form, as well as her Goddess form. You may find that one version works better for you than the other. Money rituals are very straight forward, and I have tested them all, and each one will work.

Basic Money Magick

All beings have magick to assist a magician to generate more money. Lilith is no different in this aspect. As a Goddess, she can assist you in increasing your income through established channels.

For this ritual, you'll need the Money Draw Oil, gold candles (or green), the Money Draw Sigil, six small coins, and some time.

This ritual has you bury the coins around your property

once you have finished the main part of the ritual. This magick uses the power of Gaia to assist in drawing money to you. ANY six coins will work. In the US, use pennies.

The petition can read something like: "Goddess Lilith! I ask that you enchant me so that I am a money magnet. All that I touch turns to gold! Enchant this candle to draw money to me, power these coins to funnel money to me! I call for money, and money flows to me in ever increasing amounts! Thank you, most powerful and mighty Goddess Lilith!"

Items needed:
> Lilith's candles
> Goddess Sigil
> Your petition
> Money Draw Sigil
> Incense
> Gold candle
> Offering
> Offering bowl
> Money Draw Oil
> Six small coins

Steps:

Anoint the gold candle: Put a small drop of the Money Draw Oil into the palm of your hand. Draw this oil on the gold candle, pulling it from the bottom to the top. Place the gold candle in a sturdy candle holder, and work the rest of the ritual.

Anoint the Money Draw Sigil as well. Just a small drop in the center.

Altar candles lit.

Incense lit

Lights off

Cast circle

Banishment of negative energies

Invocation to Goddess Lilith

Goddess Lilith! Hear me!

I invoke you!

For I wish your presence in my sacred space.

Lilith, Goddess of Light. Goddess of Beauty

Goddess of Empowerment!

Thy whose lips are rose red, whose kiss is as sweet as wine!

Be with me!

You have had many forms throughout time

Grace me with your presence.

At this point, look for the subtle signals that Lilith is near.

Present your case. Read your petition.

Pick up the ritual candle, and hold it up.

"Goddess Lilith, I ask that you now enchant this candle to bring to me large sums of money, in ever increasing amounts, in ways both expected and unexpected, with safety for all."

Light the candle and place it on her sigil.

Activate the Money Draw Sigil by passing it through the incense smoke while saying:

"Goddess Lilith, I now ask that you enchant this symbol to bring about the income flow I desire."

Pause a few minutes, and meditate on your desired outcome. See it happening. Focus on both the images and feelings you have when your desire manifests.

Once the sigil is enchanted, you pick up the offering, and say:

"Goddess Lilith, I humbly offer you this _____ for attending to my prayers."

Put the offering into the offering bowl, and place this on her sigil, next to the Ritual Candle.

Pick up the coins, and hold them in both hands. Imagine *golden energy* flowing into your hands and into the coins, and say:

"Into these coins, Lilith now sends gold and money magnetic energy! Money now flows to me, in ever greater amounts. These coins now draw money and wealth to me! So it is written, so it is done!"

Now close the ritual as follows:

"Goddess Lilith, your energy fills me with your loving grace. I adore you with all my being. Our work here is now done. I now say, you may depart, and please come again when I next call upon you!"

Allow the offering to remain on her sigil overnight. Then discard outside.

Pick up the coins, and go outside. Bury or hide a coin in each corner of your yard outside, or inside an apartment or condo. Once you have a coin in all four corners, bury one coin at the beginning of the walkway to your front door, then one right at the front door. Hide the coins if you can't bury them, so no one takes them.

Money Bags Ritual

This is literally what this ritual brings.

Bags of money.

This money ritual uses Lilith in her aspect of Goddess. It works a bit softer than the daemonic version. It can be combined with the success ritual, as long as you work them on separate days.

This ritual relies upon mental visualization, and the petition and desire spoken aloud.

Ritual items needed:

Altar candles, Pink and White.

Candles for money: Gold, Green, or silver

"Money" incense, usually frankincense with crushed cloves and cinnamon. If using stick incense, pick a decent "Money Draw" incense.

Money Draw oil (see appendix)

Your petition to Lilith

Offering to Goddess Lilith: fresh citrus fruit, fresh flowers, sweet breads.

Props such as photos of stacks of money, plastic coins, toy money bags. (*Optional)

To summon Lilith in her aspect of the Goddess, the physical ritual is as follows:

Place Lilith's Goddess Sigil in the center of the altar

Start incense and light altar candles.

Lights out.

Cast the circle.

Summon Lilith as Goddess, say the following:

Goddess Lilith! Hear me!

I invoke you!

For I wish your presence in my sacred space.

Lilith, Goddess of Light. Goddess of Beauty.

Goddess of Empowerment!

Thy whose lips are rose red, whose kiss is as sweet as wine!

Be with me!

You have had many forms throughout time

Grace me with your presence.

Wait a few moments, watch for the signs she is near.

Pick up your petition, address Lilith, and speak aloud your petition.

"Dear Lilith….

End this petition with a phrase such as *"As it is written as it is done!"*

Pause for a few breaths and visualize the desire occurring. Go into detail and don't worry if you're taking too long. Just visualize.

Pick up the money candle, and place a few drops of oil on it. Use both hands and gently draw the oil onto the candle.

Set the candle into its holder and say:

"Goddess Lilith, I now ask you to bless this candle to bring me (restate your desire)!"

Light the candle and place it near the petition.

Once this is done, pick up the offering and hold it up over your altar.

Say the following:

"Goddess Lilith! I give my heartfelt thanks to you for appearing and listening to my prayers of request. In gratitude, I humbly offer you this _____"

Place the offering on the Goddess sigil.

At this point, pause and take a few deep breaths.

Hold your hands over the petition and say (as strongly as you can):

"Into this petition and candle, I now project power drawn from Lilith and drawn from within me. All that I have asked for shall now manifest for me! So be it!"

It's now time to end the ritual. Do so by using her common dismissal statement:

"Goddess Lilith! I thank you again for attending to my prayers. I ask now that you depart with peace and love. And so it is!"

This ritual is now complete. Room lights on, and all but the money draw candle is extinguished.

Allow the offering to stay on the altar overnight, then dispose of it outside.

Goddess Money Bags Pathworking

This is a mental only ritual. All you need is a few moments of peace and not be disturbed.

If possible, lower the room lights.

Contact Goddess Lilith by visualizing:

A bright day, clear blue sky above.

Green grass spreads out under your feet.

A clear bubble appears in the blue sky above you.

It drifts closer. And closer.

It turns bright gold, solidifying.

Goddess Lilith appears in the golden light.

She smiles.

You now say, out loud or in your mind,

"Goddess, I thank you for coming to my aid.

"I ask that this now occur,"

Visualize bags of cash appearing around you.

A large amount of loose cash now flows down and around you.

Hold on this visual for several breaths. Then visualize:

The goddess holds up the large gold bubble. As she lifts the bubble,

Money bursts out of the bubble, flowing at you.

The money drifts and falls all around you, piling up higher and higher.

Goddess Lilith will hold this up for a few moments, and then she smiles at you.

Thank the Goddess by visualizing the following:

Hold your hands out and form a PINK ball of energy.

The energy of love and gratitude.

Gently send this ball to the Goddess and watch it swell and engulf the goddess.

At this time, Lilith will depart. See the following:

Goddess Lilith now fades into the ball of pink energy. The ball drifts up into the blue sky,

And it slowly fades from view.

This ritual is now complete.

Take a few deep breaths and return to your usual activities.

CHAPTER FIFTEEN

Love Magick

No book on Goddess magick is complete without a chapter on Love. Either finding it, enhancing it, recovering it, or just attracting it, love is one of our most treasured emotions.

The difference between Lilith's goddess love magick and the daemon sex magick is the difference between lust and love. Try not to confuse the two. In the past, I have. I must have wasted countless time in pursuing someone, all while thinking I was in love, only to find out it was lust.

Love magick is designed for a long-term effect. If all you want is the physical act, go back to the beginning of this book and work with those rituals.

Basic Love Ritual

This ritual is designed to be modified by the magician to cover multiple purposes. You can use the ritual to attract someone in specific, but unlike the sex-slave ritual, this one doesn't compel the person to love you, it just sets up the correct conditions. The rest will be up to you.

I have found this magick to be quite simple, effective, and depressing. This is because you may be so focused on a specific person, you wind up overlooking someone who is your actual soul-mate. If you simply wish to work a love ritual to attract the "perfect" mate, it's best to define those traits this person needs to have. It has to be mentioned that often, soul-mates are people who we meet who assist us in growing, or learning. Sometimes this person winds up being someone who will trigger you, and force you to make hard decisions, or cause constant arguments. This all depends on what you need to experience from the point of view of your own soul.

That aside, the use of this ritual to simply attract love can put you into a situation where you might meet someone special Otherwise, it can be used to attract someone specific. This is when it can be a source of depression. I have known people who are so fixated on one particular person; they pile all their hopes and fantasies on this one individual. They will work a sex spell, a love spell, multiple love spells, and engage with various tarot readers and other psychics to find out what the other person is feeling or thinking.

This ritual will attract that person to you, but it also may utterly fail. Lilith can help you a lot, but any magick which attempts to sway another individual to your way of thinking can fail. It's the hardest type of magick, and those who utilize the darker aspects of someone like Lilith will see some success, but no deity, daemon, angel, or saint can force someone to act against their own free will for very long.

That being said (or written), here is the basic Love Ritual Template. Adjust it as you need. And good luck!

The petition can be written like this: "Lilith, I desire love. I desire the love of a good (man/woman/sexy alien...). I ask that you place me where I can meet such a person, and that this person be perfect for me in all ways."

Or... For a specific individual, word it like this: "Lilith! I desire (name) to notice me and fall in love with me." (or words to that effect.)

A sigil can be created from your petition.

Lilith's candles (pink and white)
    Goddess Sigil
    Your petition
    Sigil for the desire
    Incense
    Pink ritual candle
    Offering
    Offering bowl
    Come to me oil
    (If targeting a specific person, add their photo to the ritual)

Steps:

Light altar candles.

Incense lit

Lights off

Cast circle

Banishment of negative energies

Invocation to Goddess Lilith

Goddess Lilith! Hear me!

I invoke you!

For I wish your presence in my sacred space.

Lilith, Goddess of Light. Goddess of Beauty.

Goddess of Empowerment!

Thy whose lips are rose red, whose kiss is as sweet as wine!

Be with me!

You have had many forms throughout time

Grace me with your presence.

At this point, look for the subtle signs that Lilith is near.

Present your case. Read your petition.

If you have a photo, hold it up now and say:

"This is the person I desire. Please guide them to me."

Pick up the ritual candle, and hold it. Anoint it with Come to Me Oil.

"Goddess Lilith, I ask that you now enchant this candle to bring love to me (or bring (name) to me)."

Light the candle and place it on her sigil.

If you have created a special sigil for this desire, hold it up now.

Pass it through the incense smoke.

"Goddess Lilith, I now ask that you enchant this symbol to bring love to me (or bring (name) to me)."

Pause a few minutes, and meditate on your desired outcome. See it happening. Focus on both the images and feelings you have when your desire manifests.

Once the sigil is enchanted, you pick up the offering, and say:

"Goddess Lilith, I humbly offer you this _____ for attending to my prayers."

Put the offering into the offering bowl, and place this on her sigil, next to the Ritual Candle.

At this time, place your hand over the sigil or the petition. Now say:

"Into this sigil and petition, I now combine my own god/goddess energy with that of your Goddess energy. Together, we will alter space and time so that my reality now shifts to allow this desire to manifest! So it is written, so it is done!"

Now close the ritual as follows:

"Goddess Lilith, your energy fills me with your loving grace. I adore you with all my being. Our work here is now done. I now say, you may depart, and please come again when I next call upon you!"

Allow the offering to remain on her sigil overnight. Then discard outside.

Pathworking Love Ritual

Using the same petition as in the ceremonial ritual, this easy pathworking will call on Lilith while in a light trance state, a mental state where you are daydreaming, but way more effective than simply daydreams.

As always, settle yourself in a comfortable spot, perhaps on the couch, or laying on your bed. Make sure you won't be disturbed for several minutes, and make sure to have the written petition so you can read it during the pathworking.

Get comfortable and relax. Allow yourself to enter Alpha.

Contact Goddess Lilith by visualizing:

A bright day, clear blue sky above.

Green grass spreads out under your feet.

A clear bubble appears in the blue sky above you.

It drifts closer. And closer.

It turns bright gold, solidifying.

Goddess Lilith appears in the golden light.

She smiles.

You now say, out loud or in your mind, your petition and desire.

Take a minute to fully visualize the meeting occurring, and the other person falling in love with you.

Now say:

"Goddess, I thank you for coming to my aid. I ask that

this now occur,"

Hold that for a few moments, then visualizing PINK light surrounding you.

This PINK light activates the petition and sigil if you made one.

At this point, give thanks to Lilith for assisting you.

She will now vanish, leaving only an outline.

In your mind, turn around and walk away from the scene.

Open your eyes. Take a few moments to return to fully awakened consciousness.

This ritual is now competed.

Strengthening Love

This ritual is for those times when it seems the love in a relationship appears to be waning. It is gentle magick, designed to fan the flames of love, which may be smothering under a layer of ash. Relationships often go through cycles, from fresh passion, then into comfortable routine, but sometimes it will appear that the flames of love are diminishing. This magick will work, and Lilith, in her goddess form, will gently reawaken this love.

There are some physical steps to take with this spell, so make sure you are prepared. This ritual works best when performed on a Friday, the traditional day of Venus/Aphrodite, but it can be worked on any day of the week.

Locate some photos of yourself with your partner from

when times were better. Find any love notes or cards that were written early in the relationship.

Red rose petals are needed, which you will place in locations throughout your home, where your partner will easily find them. Place the petals to the images of earlier versions of your relationship and tie it all with pink ribbon. Take your time, and put as many roses and images together as possible.

If you cannot find roses, then use the images with just the pink ribbon.

The idea behind this is to trigger the memories in the mind of your partner.

Next step is to run this simplified Lilith ritual.

Lilith's Pink and White candles
    Goddess Sigil
    The photographs, roses and ribbon
    Incense
    Extra pink candle
    Offering
    Offering bowl

Steps:
    Light altar candles.
    Incense lit
    Lights off
    Cast circle

Banishment of negative energies

Invocation to Goddess Lilith

Goddess Lilith! Hear me!

I invoke you!

For I wish your presence in my sacred space.

Lilith, Goddess of Light. Goddess of Beauty.

Goddess of Empowerment!

Thy whose lips are rose red, whose kiss is as sweet as wine!

Be with me!

You have had many forms throughout time

Grace me with your presence.

At this point, look for the subtle signs that Lilith is near.

Present your case. Hold up one of the photographs and say,

"Lilith, I ask that you assist me in rekindling our love for each other, love which still exists, and make our love grow stronger and stronger."

Pick up the ritual candle, and hold it up.

"Goddess Lilith, I ask that you now enchant this candle to strengthen our love."

Light the candle and place it on her sigil.

Pause a few minutes, and meditate on your desired outcome. See it happening. Focus on both the images and feelings you have when your desire manifests.

Pick up the offering, and say:

"Goddess Lilith, I humbly offer you this _____ for

attending to my prayers. "

Put the offering into the offering bowl, and place this on her sigil, next to the Ritual Candle.

At this time, place your hand over the photograph(s).

Now say:

"Into this image of our love, I now combine my own god/goddess energy with that of your Goddess energy. Together, we will alter space and time so that my reality now shifts to allow this desire to manifest! So it is written, so it is done!"

Now close the ritual as follows:

"Goddess Lilith, your energy fills me with your loving grace. I adore you with all my being. Our work here is now done. I now say, you may depart, and please come again when I next call upon you!"

Allow the offering to remain on her sigil overnight. Then discard outside.

There's no pathworking version of this ritual.

Reuniting with a Lost Love

This ritual is when someone has left you, but there's still karma to be worked out. It is also used when you've lost touch with a beloved relative, and want them to make contact. It's basic return magick, but acts softly, without hurting "Free Will" or karma.

I do not recommend using this one to force someone to return once the karma is completed. This means, if the lessons are completed, this spell will probably not function as intended. To drag someone back to you, I suggest the total subjugation ritual.

For this ritual, we will also leverage the power of Gaia, the earth, by burying the custom sigil and the person's name in a spot where it will not be discovered.

My personal experience with this magick is that it works... and works well.

Preparation for this ritual is necessary. You need to use the steps outlined in the Preparing for the Ritual chapter that covers crafting a custom sigil. Leave the back blank.

Items needed:
>
> Lilith's candles
>
> Goddess Sigil
>
> Your petition
>
> Desire Sigil
>
> Incense
>
> Pink Ritual candle
>
> Offering
>
> Offering bowl
>
> Any oils necessary
>
> A small gardening trowel or shovel
>
> Access to a small patch of ground where you can dig

Steps:
>
> Altar candles lit.

Incense lit

Lights off

Cast circle

Banishment of negative energies

Invocation to Goddess Lilith

Goddess Lilith! Hear me!

I invoke you!

For I wish your presence in my sacred space.

Lilith, Goddess of Light. Goddess of Beauty.

Goddess of Empowerment!

Thy whose lips are rose red, whose kiss is as sweet as wine!

Be with me!

You have had many forms throughout time

Grace me with your presence.

At this point, look for the subtle signs that Lilith is near.

Present your case. Read your petition.

Pause a minute, visualize this person walking towards you.

Pick up the pink candle, and hold it up.

"Goddess Lilith, I ask that you now enchant this candle so that it serves as a beacon to light the way for this person: (their name). I ask that we get back together as a couple. (or get back together as a family)"

Light the candle and place it on her sigil.

Hold up the desire sigil now.

Pick up the sigil, and on the back, write this person's name three times.

Pass the sigil through the incense smoke.

"Goddess Lilith, I now ask that you enchant this symbol to assist this person in returning to me! The earth mother and your power will guide this person back to me!"

Once the sigil is enchanted, you pick up the offering, and say:

"Goddess Lilith, I humbly offer you this _____ for attending to my prayers."

Put the offering into the offering bowl, and place this on her sigil, next to the Ritual Candle.

At this time, place your hand over the sigil and petition.

Now say:

"Into these symbols, I now combine my own god/goddess energy with that of your Goddess energy. Together, we will alter space and time so that my reality now shifts to allow this desire to manifest! So it is written, so it is done!"

Now close the ritual as follows:

"Goddess Lilith, your energy fills me with your loving grace. I adore you with all my being. Our work here is now done. I now say, you may depart, and please come again when I next call upon you!"

The ritual isn't finished until you take the paper outside. Find a remote location and bury the petition and sigil as deep as you can bury it. Cover it, making sure it won't be disturbed, and then leave.

Pathworking Reuniting with a Lost Love

For this method, you will still need to create a sigil, using a simple statement of desire, such as "Lilith, please bring (name) back to me!"

Have this sigil with you when you work this path.

Contact Goddess Lilith by visualizing:

A bright day, clear blue sky above.

Green grass spreads out under your feet.

A clear bubble appears in the blue sky above you.

It drifts closer. And closer.

It turns bright gold, solidifying.

Goddess Lilith appears in the golden light.

She smiles.

You now say, out loud or in your mind, your petition and desire.

Take a minute to fully visualize the desire manifesting. Go into detail!

Now say:

"Goddess, I thank you for coming to my aid. I ask that this desire now manifests!"

Hold that for a few moments, then visualizing PINK light surrounding you.

This PINK light activates the sigil.

Open your eyes and write their name on the sigil three times.

At this point, give thanks to Lilith for assisting you.

Send this pink light to her as an energy offering.

She will now vanish, leaving only an outline.

In your mind, turn around and walk away from the scene.

Open your eyes. Take a few moments to return to fully awakened consciousness.

Once awakened, take the sigil outside, and bury is deep in a spot where it will not be disturbed.

This ritual is now competed.

Reuniting with Friends

In our world, we will often lose track of cherished friends. The reasons this occurs are many. This magick is to assist you in physically meeting with friends you've lost touch with over the years.

This magick will open up the pathways of communication. For this, we'll need a yellow candle and an orange candle to remove any obstacles to reuniting with your friends.

This is basically the previous ritual, but adjusted to reunite friends. There is no pathworking for this one, as you need the candles working for you as well

Items needed:

Lilith's candles

Goddess Sigil

Your petition

Desire Sigil

Incense

Yellow and Orange Ritual candle

Offering

Offering bowl

Any oils necessary

A small gardening trowel or shovel

Access to a small patch of ground where you can dig

Steps:

Altar candles lit.

Incense lit

Lights off

Cast circle

Banishment of negative energies

Invocation to Goddess Lilith

Goddess Lilith! Hear me!

I invoke you!

For I wish your presence in my sacred space.

Lilith, Goddess of Light. Goddess of Beauty.

Goddess of Empowerment!

Thy whose lips are rose red, whose kiss is as sweet as wine!

Be with me!

You have had many forms throughout time

Grace me with your presence.

At this point, look for the subtle signs that Lilith is near.

Present your case. Read your petition.

Pause a minute, visualize this person walking towards you.

Pick up the yellow candle, and hold it up.

"Goddess Lilith, I ask that you now enchant this candle so that it serves to open up closed communication channels between me and (name)."

Light the candle and place it on her sigil.

Now, pick up the orange candle, and hold it up.

"Goddess Lilith, I ask that you now enchant this candle so that it serves to clear the way, remove any obstacles preventing (name) and I reconnecting."

Light this candle and place it next to the yellow candle on Lilith's sigil.

Hold up the desire sigil now.

Pick up the sigil, and on the back, write this person's name three times.

Pass the sigil through the incense smoke.

"Goddess Lilith, I now ask that you enchant this symbol to assist this person in returning to me! The earth mother and your power will guide this person back to me!"

Once the sigil is enchanted, you pick up the offering, and say:

"Goddess Lilith, I humbly offer you this _____ for attending to my prayers."

Put the offering into the offering bowl, and place this on her sigil, next to the Ritual Candle.

At this time, place your hand over the sigil and petition.

Now say:

"Into these symbols, I now combine my own god/goddess energy with that of your Goddess energy. Together, we will alter space and time so that my reality now shifts to allow this desire to manifest! So it is written, so it is done!"

Now close the ritual as follows:

"Goddess Lilith, your energy fills me with your loving grace. I adore you with all my being. Our work here is now done. I now say, you may depart, and please come again when I next call upon you!"

The ritual isn't finished until you take the paper outside. Find a remote location and bury the petition and sigil as deep as you can bury it. Cover it, making sure it won't be disturbed, and then leave.

Aura of Glamor

I suggest this magick, along with any other magick, to attract someone to you. Projecting this magick will go a long way in assisting you in attracting someone.

This works on the principle of "Like Attracting Like". I discovered something interesting back in the late 1980s. When I was just married, I must have been projecting the aura of love and glamor, because I was attracting some very attractive, and interested, women. This was because of the that weird universal law, Law of Attraction.

This magick will work off this principal. By projecting glamor, love, sexuality, you attract that to you.

The Aura of Glamor can also be used to project charisma, if you wish to enchant large groups of people, such as giving an important talk, or running for political office. Actors can use this power when auditioning to help sway the casting people to hire you for a part in either a play or movie.

This is a simple physical ritual, and pathworking. I suggest using this at the same time you work any of the other love or sex magick. Perhaps practice the pathworking and incorporate it at the close of the other rituals.

The petition is very simple, and should be worded like this: "Lilith, I ask that you now adjust my energy and cause a glow of glamor around me, allowing me to project the warm glow of love for all to see."

You can also create a sigil for this, and perhaps wear it as a charm or carry on a key-chain. I suggest the statement be: "Lilith has given me the aura of glamor and desirability."

Items needed:
  Lilith's candles
  Goddess Sigil
  Your petition
  Glamor Aura sigil
  Incense

Pink ritual candle

Offering

Offering bowl

Any oils necessary

Steps:

Light altar candles.

Incense lit

Lights off

Cast circle

Banishment of negative energies

Invocation to Goddess Lilith

Goddess Lilith! Hear me!

I invoke you!

For I wish your presence in my sacred space.

Lilith, Goddess of Light. Goddess of Beauty.

Goddess of Empowerment!

Thy whose lips are rose red, whose kiss is as sweet as wine!

Be with me!

You have had many forms throughout time

Grace me with your presence.

At this point, look for the subtle signs that Lilith is near.

Present your case. Read your petition.

Spend a few minutes meditating and visualize an aura appearing around your body. The energy is pink, and it softly spreads out. It makes your skin glow; you become more and more glamorous.

Allow this visual to continue, and pick up the pink ritual candle, and hold it up.

"Goddess Lilith, I ask that you now enchant this candle to enhance my glamor and desirability. I am unstoppable. The glow of love flows around me and through me."

Light the candle and place it on her sigil.

If you have a dedicated sigil for this desire, hold it up now.

Pass it through the incense smoke.

"Goddess Lilith, I now ask that you enchant this symbol to enhance my glamor, so that I may attract others."

Pause a few minutes, and meditate on your desired outcome. See it happening. Focus on both the images and feelings you have when your desire manifests.

Once the sigil is enchanted, you pick up the offering, and say:

"Goddess Lilith, I humbly offer you this _____ for attending to my prayers."

Put the offering into the offering bowl, and place this on her sigil, next to the Ritual Candle.

At this time, place your hand over the sigil or the petition. Now say:

"Into this sigil, I project power, my own god/goddess energy combined with that of your Goddess energy. Together, we will alter space and time so that my reality now shifts! So it is written, so it is done!"

Now close the ritual as follows:

"Goddess Lilith, your energy fills me with your loving grace. I adore you with all my being. Our work here is now done. I now say, you may depart, and please come again when I next call upon you!"

Allow the offering to remain on her sigil overnight. Then discard outside.

Pathworking

This ritual is perfect for pathworking, as it relies on visualization more than anything else. Yes, you do the ceremonial stuff with candles and all, but the core of the magick is the visualizing you perform while in the ritual.

So, with this pathworking, we skip all that and go straight to the magick Aura of Glamor.

Contact Goddess Lilith by visualizing:

A bright day, clear blue sky above.

Green grass spreads out under your feet.

A clear bubble appears in the blue sky above you.

It drifts closer. And closer.

It turns bright gold, solidifying.

Goddess Lilith appears in the golden light.

She smiles.

You now say, out loud or in your mind,

"Goddess, I thank you for coming to my aid.

"I ask that I am now filled with the aura of love. The glow of glamor now surrounds me, allowing me to project the warm glow of love for all to see."

Spend a moment seeing a pale pink light emerging from our heart to surround your entire body. It glows and becomes dazzling.

Send a small thread of this light to Goddess Lilith in gratitude for assisting you in manifesting this aura.

Bid the Goddess farewell, for it is time to end the ritual.

She will vanish, and then you can turn around and walk away.

The ritual is now complete.

If you have a sigil for this, you can activate it by having it with you in the pathworking, and imagine a beam of pink light hitting it, causing it to activate.

"Piss or Get Off the Pot" (AKA Make Him/Her Commit)

Back in Texas, I had an elderly aunt who had a lot of funny sayings. Her favorite one was "Piss or Get off The Pot" … She used this one in traffic a lot. It means get on with it. If you are in a budding relationship, and it hasn't moved forward, it might be time to work this ritual.

I have found that when two people are in a relationship, it sometimes stagnates as they fall into a comfortable routine. I saw this with my niece, who had been dating the same guy since 9th grade. The guy was very comfortable, and it took him many years to finally "pop the question". To perhaps speed things up with you, we will work this ritual.

In this ritual, we'll be using Lilith as a Goddess, just to moderate the energy she uses on the target person. It's softer, gentler, and will make the other person think it was their idea the entire time. Sneaky.

Besides a photograph of the person, you will need a petition. Phrase it somewhat like this:

"Goddess Lilith, please fly to _____ and plant in his/her mind the time to commit is now, to attest their love for me, and assist them in moving forward in this commitment."

Then add any further statements to this to clarify your desire. You should also create a sigil for this desire. Simplify the statement to something like, "Lilith helped (their name) to fully commit to me."

After drawing the sigil, write their name on the back.

The Ritual

Although magick using Lilith can be done at any time, this ritual will benefit from the energy of Venus, so to use that energy, work this ritual between the new and full moon, and on a Friday.

Items needed:

Lilith's candles

Goddess Sigil

Your petition

Sigil for the desire

Their photograph

Incense

Pink ritual candle

Offering (Red Wine or Cake)

Offering bowl

Come To Me oil

Steps:

Place the oil on the candle and sigil

Light altar candles.

Incense lit

Lights off

Cast circle

Banishment of negative energies

Invocation to Goddess Lilith

Goddess Lilith! Hear me!

I invoke you!

For I wish your presence in my sacred space.

Lilith, Goddess of Light. Goddess of Beauty.

Goddess of Empowerment!

Thy whose lips are rose red, whose kiss is as sweet as wine!

Be with me!

You have had many forms throughout time

Grace me with your presence.

At this point, look for subtle signals that Lilith is near.

Present your case. Read your petition.

Pick up the ritual candle, and hold it up.

"Goddess Lilith, I ask that you now enchant this candle to cause (name) to commit to me."

Light the candle and place it on her sigil.

Pick up the sigil you drew.

Pass it through the incense smoke.

"Goddess Lilith, I now ask that you enchant this sigil to have (their name) commit to me."

Once the sigil is enchanted, you pick up the offering, and say:

"Goddess Lilith, I humbly offer you this _____ for attending to my prayers."

Put the offering into the offering bowl, and place this on her sigil, next to the Ritual Candle.

At this time, place your hand over the sigil or the petition.

Now say:

"Into this sigil and petition, I now combine my own god/goddess energy with that of your Goddess energy. Together, we will alter space and time so that my reality now shifts to allow this desire to manifest! So it is written, so it is done!"

Now close the ritual as follows:

"Goddess Lilith, your energy fills me with your loving grace. I adore you with all my being. Our work here is now done. I now say, you may depart, and please come again when

I next call upon you!"

Allow the offering to remain on the altar at least overnight, then discard outside.

Pathworking Commit Ritual

For this method, you will still need to create a sigil, using a simple statement of desire, such as "Lilith, please make (name) commit to me!"

Have this sigil with you when you work this path.

Contact Goddess Lilith by visualizing:

A bright day, clear blue sky above.

Green grass spreads out under your feet.

A clear bubble appears in the blue sky above you.

It drifts closer. And closer.

It turns bright gold, solidifying.

Goddess Lilith appears in the golden light.

She smiles.

You now say, out loud or in your mind, your petition and desire.

Take a minute to fully visualize the desire manifesting. Go into detail!

Now say:

"Goddess, I thank you for coming to my aid. I ask that this desire now manifests!"

Hold that for a few moments, then visualizing PINK light surrounding you.

This PINK light activates the sigil.

Open your eyes and write their name on the sigil three times.

At this point, give thanks to Lilith for assisting you.

Send this pink light to her as an energy offering.

She will now vanish, leaving only an outline.

In your mind, turn around and walk away from the scene.

Open your eyes. Take a few moments to return to fully awakened consciousness.

Once awakened, take the sigil outside, and bury it deep in a spot where it will not be disturbed.

This ritual is now competed.

CHAPTER SIXTEEN

Protect Children

Ironically, the ancient myths about Lilith portrayed her as a demon who'd slay children. In reality, the opposite is more the truth. She is a goddess for the family and will protect children from the dangers of our society in our current times.

The protection can be all pathworking, or it can activate a talisman. There is a protection sigil which can be activated and placed on the child's clothing as a design, or on their phones, worn as a necklace or other charm. It's simple and effective. I know an artist who can quickly turn this design into a beautiful small medallion. His link is in the Appendix.

The ceremonial ritual is geared towards activating the talisman, no matter if you made it using a print of the sigil, or hired an artist to craft one in pewter or bronze.

Physical Ritual to activate the Talisman

This simple ritual only needs a few things.

Lilith's Goddess Candles

Lilith's Goddess Sigil

The Talisman

Frankincense resin and burner, or stick

A simple offering

Offering Bowl

Go into your space, light the candles and cast the circle.

Summon Lilith:

Goddess Lilith! Hear me!

I invoke you!

For I wish your presence in my sacred space.

Lilith, Goddess of Light. Goddess of Beauty.

Goddess of Empowerment!

Thy whose lips are rose red, whose kiss is as sweet as wine!

Be with me!

You have had many forms throughout time

Grace me with your presence.

Pause now. Pick up the talisman, and stare at it.

Lilith! I ask that you now enchant this talisman,

So that it will now protect (name)

Pass the Talisman through the incense smoke.

Allow the smoke to engulf the Talisman.

Lilith! I give thanks to you for protecting my child(ren).

They will keep this sacred object close, reminding them
Of your loving and protective magick!

Place the offering in the bowl.

Snuff out the altar candles.

Allow the incense to burn out.

Leave the offering overnight, then place it outside.

Pathworking Activation

You'll need the sigil or talisman for this. As with the other pathworking rituals, pick a time and day when you won't be disturbed and allow yourself to go into a slight trance, or alpha, state. You can refer to this book while in the ritual.

When ready, contact Goddess Lilith by visualizing:

A bright day, clear blue sky above.

Green grass spreads out under your feet.

A clear bubble appears in the blue sky above you.

It drifts closer. And closer.

It turns bright gold, solidifying.

Goddess Lilith appears in the golden light.

She smiles.

You now say, out loud or in your mind, your desire to activate the sigil/talisman.

Lilith will now send GOLD light to you, which will enter your forehead, and then fill your body.

Allow this light to flow from your heart and into the sigil/talisman.

Take a minute to fully visualize this happening. Allow the sigil/talisman to fully glow, with the gold light glowing brighter and brighter.

After a few moments, allow the light to fade slowly.

Now say:

"Goddess, I thank you for coming and activating these symbols to keep my family safe!"

At this point, give thanks to Lilith for assisting you.

Visualize pink light beginning to glow in your heart center.

Send this pink light to her as an energy offering.

She will now vanish, leaving only an outline.

In your mind, turn around and walk away from the scene.

Open your eyes. Take a few moments to return to fully awakened consciousness.

This ritual is now competed.

Safety for your Partner/Spouse

Along with keeping your children safe, you can also have Lilith extend that protection to your partner or spouse, and other family members. The regular protection sigil is used in this, and it's a simple ritual to activate it. You could, if pressed, use the activated children's talisman, but it's best to use the dedicated protection sigil, as it's attuned to an adult's energy.

As with the Children's sigil, this can be crafted into a permanent talisman, using any material, or by hiring an artist to make one.

Physical Ritual to activate the Talisman

    This simple ritual only needs a few things.

    Lilith's Goddess Candles

    Lilith's Goddess Sigil

    The Talisman

    Frankincense resin and burner or stick

    A simple offering

    Offering Bowl

Go into your space, light the candles and cast the circle.

    Summon Lilith:

    Goddess Lilith! Hear me!

    I invoke you!

    For I wish your presence in my sacred space.

    Lilith, Goddess of Light. Goddess of Beauty.

    Goddess of Empowerment!

    Thy whose lips are rose red, whose kiss is as sweet as wine!

    Be with me!

    You have had many forms throughout time

    Grace me with your presence.

    Pause now. Pick up the talisman, and stare at it.

      Lilith! I ask that you now enchant this talisman,

      So that it will now protect (name)

    Pass the Talisman through the incense smoke.

    Allow the smoke to engulf the Talisman.

Lilith! I give thanks to you for protecting (name).
They will keep this sacred object close, reminding them
Of your loving and protective magick!

Place the offering in the bowl.

Snuff out the altar candles.

Allow the incense to burn out.

Leave the offering overnight, then place it outside.

Pathworking Safety for your Partner/Spouse

You'll need the sigil or talisman for this. As with the other pathworking rituals, pick a time and day when you won't be disturbed and allow yourself to go into a slight trance, or alpha, state. You can refer to this book while in the ritual.

When ready, contact Goddess Lilith by visualizing:

A bright day, clear blue sky above.

Green grass spreads out under your feet.

A clear bubble appears in the blue sky above you.

It drifts closer. And closer.

It turns bright gold, solidifying.

Goddess Lilith appears in the golden light.

She smiles.

You now say, out loud or in your mind, your desire to activate the sigil/talisman.

Lilith will now send GOLD light to you, which will enter your forehead, and then fill your body.

Allow this light to flow from your heart and into the sigil/talisman.

Take a minute to fully visualize this happening. Allow the sigil/talisman to fully glow, with the gold light growing brighter and brighter.

After a few moments, allow the light to fade slowly.

Now say:

"Goddess, I thank you for coming and activating these symbols to keep my family safe!"

At this point, give thanks to Lilith for assisting you.

Visualize pink light beginning to glow in your heart center.

Send this pink light to her as an energy offering.

She will now vanish, leaving only an outline.

In your mind, turn around and walk away from the scene.

Open your eyes. Take a few moments to return to fully awakened consciousness.

This ritual is now compete.

Healthy Childbirth

Having a healthy baby is paramount with most families, and Lilith can be asked to help insure this is the case, the birth of a healthy baby.

For this, use a blue candle and the usual incense and oils. Work on a Sunday or Monday, but any day of the week will work.

Craft a petition, saying something like, "Lilith! I ask that you assist me in starting (or expanding) my family. I ask that you work to make sure my child is healthy, and the birth is safe and health for us both!"

A sigil can be made using a simpler statement such as "Lilith insures I have a healthy baby." Craft the sigil in the usual way.

When ready, work the physical ritual as follows:

Items needed:

 Lilith's candles

 Goddess Sigil

 Your petition

 Sigil for a healthy child

 Incense

 Blue ritual candle

 Offering

 Offering bowl

 Any oils necessary

Steps:

 Altar candles lit.

 Incense lit

 Lights off

 Cast circle

 Banishment of negative energies

 Invocation to Goddess Lilith

 Goddess Lilith! Hear me!

I invoke you!

For I wish your presence in my sacred space.

Lilith, Goddess of Light. Goddess of Beauty

Goddess of Empowerment!

Thy whose lips are rose red, whose kiss is as sweet as wine!

Be with me!

You have had many forms throughout time

Grace me with your presence.

At this point, check to see if Lilith is near.

Present your case. Read your petition.

Pick up the ritual candle, and hold it up.

"Goddess Lilith, I ask that you now enchant this candle to see that I give birth to a healthy baby!" Go into detail here if you wish.

Light the candle and place it on her sigil.

If you have a dedicated sigil for this desire, hold it up now.

Pass it through the incense smoke.

"Goddess Lilith, I now ask that you enchant this symbol to bring about the birth of a healthy baby."

Pause a few minutes, and meditate on your desired outcome. See it happening. Focus on both the images and feelings you have when your desire manifests.

Once the sigil is enchanted, you pick up the offering, and say:

"Goddess Lilith, I humbly offer you this _____ for

attending to my prayers."

Put the offering into the offering bowl, and place this on her sigil, next to the Ritual Candle.

At this time, place your hand over the sigil or the petition.

Now say:

"Into this sigil, candle and petition, I now combine my own god/goddess energy with that of your Goddess energy. Together, we will alter space and time so that my reality now shifts to allow this desire to manifest! So it is written, so it is done!"

Now close the ritual as follows:

"Goddess Lilith, your energy fills me with your loving grace. I adore you with all my being. Our work here is now done. I now say, you may depart, and please come again when I next call upon you!"

Allow the offering to remain on her sigil overnight. Then discard outside.

Pathworking for Healthy Childbirth

Use the petition and sigil from the physical ritual.

When ready, contact Goddess Lilith by visualizing:

A bright day, clear blue sky above.

Green grass spreads out under your feet.

A clear bubble appears in the blue sky above you.

It drifts closer. And closer.

It turns bright gold, solidifying.

Goddess Lilith appears in the golden light.

She smiles.

You now say, out loud or in your mind, your petition and desire.

Take a minute to fully visualize the desire manifesting. Go into detail!

Now say:

"Goddess, I thank you for coming to my aid. I ask that this now occur,"

Hold that for a few moments, then visualizing PINK light surrounding you.

This PINK light activates the petition and sigil if you made one.

At this point, give thanks to Lilith for assisting you.

Send this pink light to her as an energy offering.

She will now vanish, leaving only an outline.

In your mind, turn around and walk away from the scene.

Open your eyes. Take a few moments to return to fully awakened consciousness.

This ritual is now competed.

Success in School

Many daemons have "secret knowledge" as one of their powers. Lilith is big on sharing knowledge, so much so, she has appeared in myths about being the one who gave Eve the fruit from the tree of knowledge. We're working with Lilith in her

Goddess form, as she works with softer magick as a goddess, versus being a serious taskmaster when in her daemoness form.

Success in school can be worked for yourself, a family member, or anyone else. You will need an item of their clothing or something with their handwriting on it to insure the magick connects properly. With your children, you should use one of their "primary" teeth, or baby teeth, to connect them to this magick.

Along with that, you will need a petition. It can be worded very simply: "Goddess Lilith, you who bestowed knowledge upon Eve and all of her descendants, I ask that you now assist ("me", or their name) in their (my) efforts in school. See to it they/me retain the knowledge to excel on all exams, and that I am/they are very successful!"

Reduce this statement down to something like "I/(name) is successful in school" for a sigil.

Use a yellow candle for "communication", and a good choice of incense would be frankincense. No particular day of the week is best, so work this when it is convenient.

Items needed:
    Lilith's candles
    Goddess Sigil
    Your petition
    The sigil you made
    Incense
    Yellow ritual candle

Offering

Offering bowl

Any oils you feel are needed

Steps:

Altar candles lit.

Incense lit

Lights off

Cast circle

Banishment of negative energies

Invocation to Goddess Lilith

Goddess Lilith! Hear me!

I invoke you!

For I wish your presence in my sacred space.

Lilith, Goddess of Light. Goddess of Beauty

Goddess of Empowerment!

Thy whose lips are rose red, whose kiss is as sweet as wine!

Be with me!

You have had many forms throughout time

Grace me with your presence.

At this point, check for signs Lilith is near.

Present your case. Read your petition.

Pick up the ritual candle, and hold it up.

"Goddess Lilith, I ask that you now enchant this candle to ensure success in school for (name) (myself)."

Light the candle and place it on her sigil.

If you have a dedicated sigil for this desire, hold it up now. Pass it through the incense smoke.

"Goddess Lilith, I now ask that you enchant this symbol to bring about success in school for (myself) (name)."

Pause a few minutes, and meditate on your desired outcome. See it happening. Focus on both the images and feelings you have when your desire manifests.

Once the sigil is enchanted, you pick up the offering, and say:

"Goddess Lilith, I humbly offer you this _____ for attending to my prayers."

Put the offering into the offering bowl, and place this on her sigil, next to the Ritual Candle.

At this time, place your hand over the sigil or the petition. Now say:

"Into these images and symbols I now combine my own god/goddess energy with that of your Goddess energy. Together, we will alter space and time so that my reality now shifts to allow this desire to manifest! So it is written, so it is done!"

Now close the ritual as follows:

"Goddess Lilith, your energy fills me with your loving grace. I adore you with all my being. Our work here is now done. I now say, you may depart, and please come again when I next call upon you!"

Allow the offering to remain on her sigil overnight. Then

discard outside.

Pathworking Success in School

Use the same petition and sigil from the physical ritual. Then, when ready, contact Goddess Lilith by visualizing:

A bright day, clear blue sky above.

Green grass spreads out under your feet.

A clear bubble appears in the blue sky above you.

It drifts closer. And closer.

It turns bright gold, solidifying.

Goddess Lilith appears in the golden light.

She smiles.

You now say, out loud or in your mind, your petition and desire.

Take a minute to fully visualize the desire manifesting. Go into detail!

Now say:

"Goddess, I thank you for coming to my aid."

"I ask that this now occur!"

Visualize the outcome AGAIN.

Hold that for a few moments, then visualizing PINK light surrounding you.

This PINK light activates the petition and sigil if you made one.

At this point, give thanks to Lilith for assisting you.

Send this pink light to her as an energy offering.

She will now vanish, leaving only an outline.

In your mind, turn around and walk away from the scene.

Open your eyes. Take a few moments to return to fully awakened consciousness.

This ritual is now competed.

CHAPTER SEVENTEEN

Healing Magick

Healing yourself or a loved one physically.

DISCLAIMER

This is not meant to be a substitute for actual medical treatment. This magic is designed to work through medical systems. A new doctor, a new test, the actual issue being relieved via treatment.

That being said, let's look at what Lilith can do in this area.

We'll deal with the physical body and its health first, then into emotional health, including grief and sorrow.

With physical healing, Lilith will direct energy into the target, either yourself, or a friend or loved one. This energy is typically blue, but Lilith says we're going to be using a pinkish/reddish energy.

It is my assertion that many physical illnesses have a

spiritual origin. Negative energy will swirl around our etheric bodies, often lodging in the energy. Once there, the negativity will begin to "seep" into our physical body, causing pain and illness. I do know that fear is a powerful emotion associated with illness. Allowing fear to consume your life results in illness of one type or another. Illnesses are often fear based, triggered by the negative energy of worry. Worry is just negative magick.

For many, the idea of health problems is associated with a fear of medical expenses. We'll deal with that, by using magick to make the treatments available.

So let's begin with a ritual for physically healing.

Physical Healing

First, determine what might be preventing you from being well. Finances? Proper medical treatment? Access to treatment? Perhaps the issue is finding the right doctors?

It will start with resources! This is a term can cover all of the above, so we'll use it as our main statement.

The petition will read a lot like this: "Great Goddess Lilith! I ask now that you bring to me the resources to assist me in gaining full physical health!"

Phrasing this particular way will by-pass the tricky "human spirits are fully healthy" curve-ball often throw at us when working magick for health. (*Spirit ALWAYS says we're healthy, because our soul is healthy, regardless of our physical condition. Your body might be dead, but YOU are fine.) Of course, you should word this in a way that fits your situation. Also, consider creating a sigil from this desire.

For the ritual itself, many sources suggest working on a Monday, and it's the same with Lilith.

Items needed:
 Lilith's candles
 Goddess Sigil
 Your petition
 Pink Candle
 Incense
 Offering
 Offering bowl
 Aromatic oils, such as Lavender, Clove, or Sandalwood

Steps:
 Altar candles lit.
 Incense lit
 Lights off
 Cast circle
 Banishment of negative energies
 Invocation to Goddess Lilith
 Goddess Lilith! Hear me!
 I invoke you!
 For I wish your presence in my sacred space.
 Lilith, Goddess of Light. Goddess of Beauty

Goddess of Empowerment!

Thy whose lips are rose red, whose kiss is as sweet as wine!

Be with me!

You have had many forms throughout time

Grace me with your presence.

At this point, look for the subtle signs that Lilith is near.

Present your case. Read your petition.

Pick up the ritual candle, and place a few small drops of oil on it, then hold it up.

"Goddess Lilith, I ask that you now enchant this candle to bring me the resources to obtain full physical health!"

Light the candle and place it on her sigil.

If you have a dedicated sigil for this desire, hold it up now.

Pass it through the incense smoke.

"Goddess Lilith, I now ask that you enchant this symbol to bring about healing me physically."

Pause a few minutes, and meditate on your desired outcome. See it happening. Focus on both the images and feelings you have when your desire manifests.

Once the sigil is enchanted, you pick up the offering, and say:

"Goddess Lilith, I humbly offer you this _____ for attending to my prayers."

Put the offering into the offering bowl, and place this on her sigil, next to the Ritual Candle.

At this time, place your hand over the sigil or the petition. Now say:

"Into this sigil and petition, I now combine my own god/goddess energy with that of your Goddess energy. Together, we will alter space and time so that my reality now shifts to allow this desire to manifest! So it is written, so it is done!"

Now close the ritual as follows:

"Goddess Lilith, your energy fills me with your loving grace. I adore you with all my being. Our work here is now done. I now say, you may depart, and please come again when I next call upon you!"

Allow the offering to remain on her sigil overnight. Then discard outside.

Pathworking Healing Magick

We'll use the same sigil and petition to work this version of the ritual. When ready, go into alpha, and contact Goddess Lilith by visualizing:

A bright day, clear blue sky above.

Green grass spreads out under your feet.

A clear bubble appears in the blue sky above you.

It drifts closer. And closer.

It turns bright gold, solidifying.

Goddess Lilith appears in the golden light.

She smiles.

You now say, out loud or in your mind, your petition and

desire.

Take a minute to fully visualize the desire manifesting. Go into detail!

Now say:

"Goddess, I thank you for coming to my aid."

"I ask that this now occur,"

Hold that for a few moments, then visualizing PINK light surrounding you.

This PINK light activates the petition and sigil if you made one.

At this point, give thanks to Lilith for assisting you.

Send this pink light to her as an energy offering.

She will now vanish, leaving only an outline.

In your mind, turn around and walk away from the scene.

Open your eyes. Take a few moments to return to fully awakened consciousness.

This ritual is now compete.

Healing Emotionally

This also covers mental health, and the issues associated with mental traumas. This includes grief, mourning over loss, and trauma from abusive relationships. This is designed to work along with traditional treatments.

(*Disclaimer! Seek professional help to assist with all traumas, and seek counseling for abusive situations, including domestic abuse.)

With this, we will use the color "aqua", or a light blue candle. If you can't find one, go with white or yellow. The suggested oils are honeysuckle, lavender, frankincense, and chamomile. Work this on a Monday or Thursday.

The petition will be worded similar to the petition for physical health: "Great Goddess Lilith! I seek your assistance in finding the resources and help to bring to me mental calmness, mental health, and emotional wellness."

If dealing with loss and grief, word it like this: "Great Goddess Lilith! I ask now that you bring me peace from my sorrows, assist me in healing my grief. Show me that all will be okay, I ask you to cover me in your love!"

Work this into a custom sigil if you can. Then carry it with you until you have healed emotionally.

Items needed:
    Lilith's candles
    Goddess Sigil
    Your petition
    Sigil for healing
    Incense
    Light blue or aqua ritual candle
    Offering
    Offering bowl
    Any oils necessary

Steps:

Altar candles lit.

Incense lit

Lights off

Cast circle

Banishment of negative energies

Invocation to Goddess Lilith

Goddess Lilith! Hear me!

I invoke you!

For I wish your presence in my sacred space.

Lilith, Goddess of Light. Goddess of Beauty

Goddess of Empowerment!

Thy whose lips are rose red, whose kiss is as sweet as wine!

Be with me!

You have had many forms throughout time

Grace me with your presence.

At this point, look for the subtle signs that Lilith is near.

Read your petition. State your case and ask for help.

Pick up the ritual candle, and hold it up.

"Goddess Lilith, I ask that you now enchant this candle to help ease my mental anguish and bring to me the resources I need!" describing your desire

Light the candle and place it on her sigil.

If you have a dedicated sigil for this desire, hold it up now.

Pass it through the incense smoke.

"Goddess Lilith, I now ask that you enchant this symbol to bring the resources I need to achieve mental wellness."

Pause a few minutes, and meditate on your desired outcome. See it happening. Focus on both the images and feelings you have when your desire manifests.

Once the sigil is enchanted, you pick up the offering, and say:

"Goddess Lilith, I humbly offer you this _____ for attending to my prayers."

Put the offering into the offering bowl, and place this on her sigil, next to the Ritual Candle.

At this time, place your hand over the sigil or the petition.

Now say:

"Into this sigil and petition, I now combine my own god/goddess energy with that of your Goddess energy. Together, we will alter space and time so that my reality now shifts to allow this desire to manifest! So it is written, so it is done!"

Now close the ritual as follows:

"Goddess Lilith, your energy fills me with your loving grace. I adore you with all my being. Our work here is now done. I now say, you may depart, and please come again when I next call upon you!"

Allow the offering to remain on her sigil overnight. Then discard outside.

Pathworking Healing Emotionally

We'll use the same petition and sigil used in the physical ritual. Find a good time, make sure you won't be disturbed.

Enter into a trance, alpha state of mind, then contact Goddess Lilith by visualizing:

A bright day, clear blue sky above.

Green grass spreads out under your feet.

A clear bubble appears in the blue sky above you.

It drifts closer. And closer.

It turns bright gold, solidifying.

Goddess Lilith appears in the golden light.

She smiles.

You now say, out loud or in your mind, your petition and desire.

Take a minute to fully visualize the desire manifesting. Go into detail!

Now say:

"Goddess, I thank you for coming to my aid."

"I ask that this now occur,"

Hold that for a few moments, then visualizing PINK light surrounding you.

This PINK light activates the petition and sigil if you made one.

At this point, give thanks to Lilith for assisting you.

Send this pink light to her as an energy offering.

She will now vanish, leaving only an outline.

In your mind, turn around and walk away from the scene.

Open your eyes. Take a few moments to return to fully awakened consciousness.

This ritual is now competed.

CHAPTER EIGHTEEN

The Sigils

Daemoness Lilith (complex)

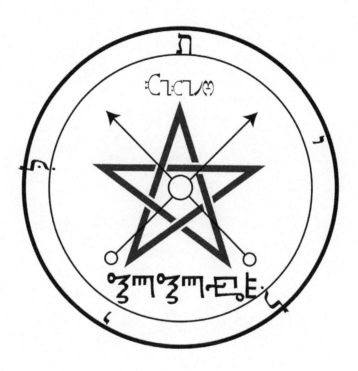

Daemoness Lilith (Simple)

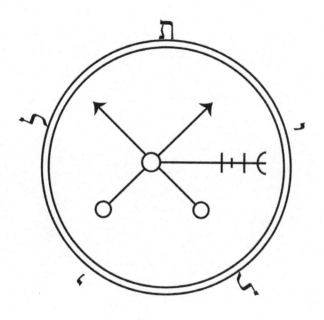

Goddess Lilith

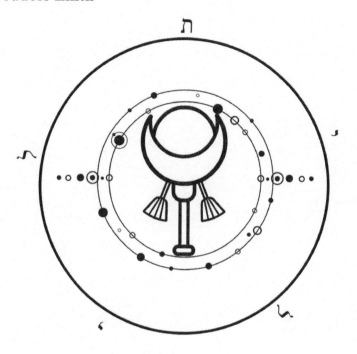

Goddess Lilith (Simple)

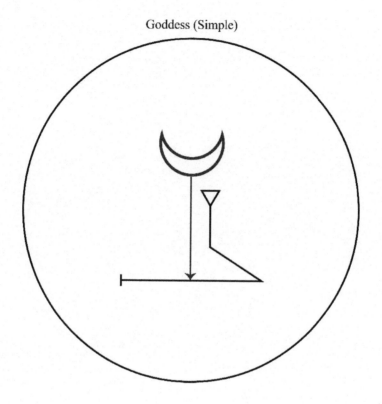

Goddess (Simple)

Protect Children

Lilith Protects Child

Protection Sigil

Money Draw

Money Draw

Compel Sigil

Compel

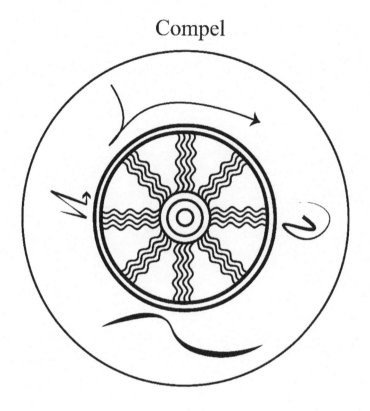

Success Sigil

Success

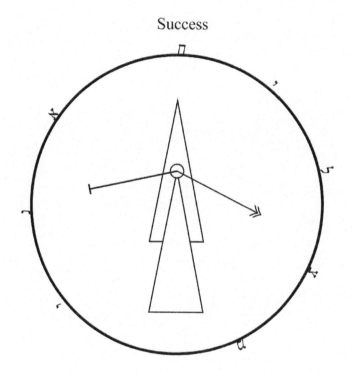

DAVID THOMPSON

APPENDIX

Helpful Links

Links to the Sigils in this book, as well as Pendulum worksheets:

https://davepsychic.com/lilithsigils/

The Talimancer: https://www.facebook.com/thetalimancer1

Oils

Most oils can be purchased through any online occult website, or in person. If you desire, you can craft your own. Below are some common recipes for magick oils. (*I personally buy all my oils, except for the "Come To Me Oil")

Command Oil

In a base of mineral oil, blend the following ingredients:

Essential oil of bergomot

Licorice root

Calamus root

Few bits of frankincense

Top off with honeysuckle or rose oil for fragrance

Allow the mixture to steep for 30 days in a cool dark place. Then, you can use as is or strain it into another container.

Come to me oil:

1/4 cup base oil

2 drops rose geranium

2 drops Oil of sweetpea.

Herbs to add:

rose petals

Queen Elizbeth root

patchouli leaf

Mix, cap in a small bottle and let set a few weeks.

(This recipe was given to me by my granny, who was sort of a witch herself. Mid-wife in the 1920s and 1930s to neighboring farms in north Texas. I tried this oil one Friday night when I was in college, and I attracted several women throughout the evening. I simply placed a single drop on my neck.)

<u>Crown of Success Oil:</u>

    1/4 cup base oil

      Vetiver

      Bay Leaf

      Gold Glitter / Pyrite etc.

    Essential oils:

      Bergamot

      Frankincense

      Sandalwood

      Cinnamon

Mis equal parts of each into the base oil, and allow it to sit for several weeks in a tightly stoppered bottle.

<u>Money Draw Oil</u>

    1/4 cup base oil

      Pine oil

      Basel oil

      Clove oil

      Cinnamon Oil

      Gold glitter

Put a few drops of each into the base oil. Add some glitter. Shake. Can substitute peppermint for Pine. Cap tightly and anoint candles, sigils, etc.

Misc Items:

Black Salt:

Place some rosemary, thyme, and a bay leaf into a old sauce pan.

Turn on your stove and purposely burn the herbs, until they are turned into black ash.

Remove the burnt herbs and place into a grinder or a mortar and pestle.

Add a few spoons of table salt.

Grind it all together.

Store in a small jar or bottle.

DO NOT buy or use the black salt used for cooking.

You can also take a piece of coal, powder it and mix with salt.

The Pendulum

Don't happen to have a Pendulum? No worries! No sense in making this harder than it is. Don't over think. Just make a pendulum!

A pendulum can be made from most anything. All you really need is a length of string or jewelry chain, and something to tie at the bottom.

You can use a ring, a small stone, or even a house key.

Just attach the ring or key to the end of the string or

chain, and TA DAH! A pendulum! Wasn't that EASY?
Simpler *IS* better!

Activating and Charging your Pendulum

Before working the ritual that uses a pendulum, let's
first consecrate the pendulum.

To do this, place the pendulum on your workspace and
hold your hands over it.

Imagine a light entering your head and flowing into
your hands, then into the pendulum.

Now say:

**In the name of EH-EI-EH I ask you, Angel
METATRON to bless this pendulum and shape its
energies for spirit communication with Genius entities.
Make it safe for myself while I use this pendulum. So be it!
Amein!** (That last work is Hebraic for So be IT)

Now, your pendulum is ready for use.

Pendulum Charts

Alphabet Chart

Yes/No Chart

Write in your own answers

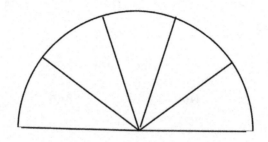

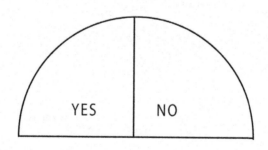

Pendulum Wheel Dates

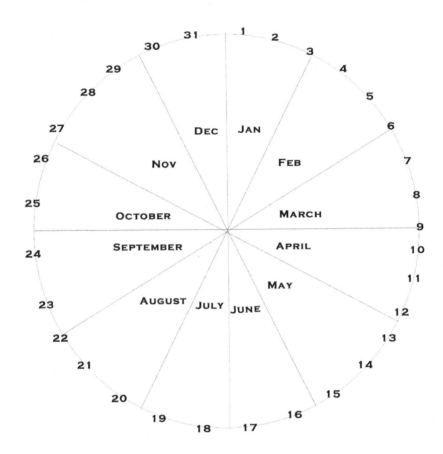

Full size charts available online – see the links.

Banishment

A.K.A. Modified Banishment of the Pentagram

Stand in the center of your room facing east.

Relax. Stand with arms at your side.

First thing reconnect to the universe.

Imagine growing larger and larger. Your point of view rises towards the ceiling in your space, and out above your house (unless you are outside)

Now, imagine you are raising above your neighborhood. Keep growing larger and larger.

You rise above the entire area, then keep growing and rise above the town. Then you are so high, you begin to see the entire earth. Keep rising up as you now speed past our Sun, and further out until all you see is the galaxy, its magnificent arms spreading out in every direction.

Keep growing and rising until above you appears a huge funnel, with streamers of colorful light flowing all around. Soak in this energy, allow the energy to fill you.

Breathing slowly, bring yourself back to your space.

Close your eyes and raise your right hand above your head, pointing at the ceiling with a finger

Say:

"You are"

With your arm straight, swing your hand in front of you

until you are pointing at the floor between your feet

Say:

"This Universe."

Still pointing at the floor, bend your elbow and bring your hand up until you are pointing at your right shoulder

Say;

"The Power"

Move your hand across your chest and point at your left shoulder

Say:

"And The Glory"

Bring both palms together to your chest (as if in prayer)

Say:

"Forever, So be it"

Return your left hand to the side and point directly in front of you with your right hand (like pointing at the rising sun or moon)

Make a small circle in front of you, clockwise and say:

"Tetra"

Now, move to face the south, and repeat the circle and say:

"Gram"

Again, move to face the west and make the small circle, saying;

"Mut"

Turn to the north, and repeat the circle motion, saying:

"Ton"

Turn so that you are facing east again.

Using the finger of your right hand, make a huge STAR in the air in front of you

Now say:

"I send from this place all intruding forces. They shall go far away and be powerless to interfere with my wishes, my thoughts, or my emotion. So be It"

ABOUT THE AUTHOR

Dave is an author of adult fantasy (The Furies series) as well as author of occult books about magick.

David began working ritual magick back in the 1970s. He took a brief break, then used the power of this magick to create a photography career which took him to Los Angeles and work as a photographer for multiple magazines.

David has studied magick in all forms, and in 2018, released a three-part magick instruction course in High Magick. Thousands of students have benefited from David's unique teaching style, making ceremonial magick accessible to everyone.

This book on Lilith is book 5 in his High Magick Series.

Dave also has a series on Grecian Magick, exploring the aspects of ceremonial magick with the gods and goddesses of ancient Greece.

Dave's Facebook Page:
https://www.facebook.com/DavePsychic/

Secrets of Magick Facebook Group:
https://www.facebook.com/groups/secretsofmagick

Join the Grecian Magick Facebook group!
https://www.facebook.com/groups/grecianmagick

Dave's Etsy page for Magick themed merchandise:
https://www.etsy.com/shop/HighMagik101

And finally, Dave's webpage, book readings and his services:
https://davepsychic.com

Sign-up for my Newsletter and get a FREE E-Book!
https://davepsychic.com/newsletter

Magick Books by David Thompson

Available as EPUB, Paperback and Hardcover (*)

High Magick Series
- High Magick 101
- Daemons of High Magick
- Daemons and the Law of Attraction*

- Magick of Astaroth*

Grecian Magick Series
- Magick of Apollo
- Magick of Hermes
- Magick of Aphrodite
- Magick of Fortuna*
- Greco-Roman Wealth Magick*
- Magick of the Sirens/Magick of the Muses

Fiction Novels by David Thompson

The Furies Series
- Angels of Vengeance
- Descent into Tartarus
- Furies: Beginnings
- Brianna: Making of a Fury

Made in the USA
Monee, IL
26 June 2023

37642799R00134